Other Translations by Thomas Cleary

THE
BOOK OF
BALANCE AND
HARMONY

Translated and with
an Introduction by
Thomas Cleary

1989
NORTH POINT PRESS
San Francisco

90-1934

Copyright © 1989 Thomas Cleary
Printed in the United States of America

LIBRARY OF CONGRESS
CATALOGING-IN-PUBLICATION DATA

Li, Tao-ch'un.
   [Chung ho chi. English]
   The Book of balance and harmony / translated and
   with an introduction by Thomas Cleary.
      p.   cm.
   Translation of: Chung ho chi.
   ISBN 0-86547-363-3 (pbk.)
   1. Taoism. I. Cleary, Thomas F., 1949–   . II. Title.
BL 1923.L5313   1989   89-2895
299'.514—dc19

CONTENTS

INTRODUCTION

The Book of Balance and Harmony is a famous anthology of writings by a thirteenth-century Taoist master of the School of Complete Reality, a movement begun a thousand years ago to restore the original principles and practices of Taoism. This collection, compiled by one of the master's disciples and still current in Taoist circles of East Asia, provides a most unusual compendium of the teachings of Complete Reality Taoism, including its theoretical and practical basis in classical Taoism.

Taoism is very difficult to define. Not only is the object of its attention by nature indefinable, but the manner of its expression varies so greatly that there is no conceptual framework that will encompass all the manifestations of thought and action commonly referred to as Taoist. Such unity as one finds in Taoism is believed by Taoists to be an internal rather than external coherence, a common source of inspiration and knowledge that expresses itself in any number of ways according to the circumstances in which it operates.

In this respect—the idea of inner unity in spite of outward diversity—Taoism closely resembles Buddhism and Sufism, both of which share many other points of similarity. Like Buddhism and Sufism, Taoism has produced giants in virtually every field of human endeavor and lays claim to practical knowledge of the deepest secrets of mind and matter. The passage of time and the acquisition of knowledge through material science have if anything substantiated this claim to higher knowledge, even if they have not uncovered the most important point: the means by which this knowledge was acquired by the mystical scientists of ancient times.

The general idea of the Tao is beyond a doubt the most fundamental and pervasive concept to be found in Chinese thought, and as such it lends itself to use in almost any context. According to *Huainanzi*, one of the better-known classics of Taoism, the Tao is "that by virtue of which mountains are high, that by virtue of which oceans are deep, that by virtue of which animals run, that by virtue of which birds fly, that by virtue of which the sun and moon are bright." In short, the Tao is the general and specific law of the universe. Everything has its Tao, and every Tao is a reflection of the Great Tao, the universal Tao that underlies all things. So comprehensive is the meaning of the Tao that Confucius, the great educator, was able to say of the inconceivable fulfillment its understanding brings, "Hear the Tao in the morning, and you may well die that night."

It would, however, be oversimplifying matters to say that the totality of the bewildering variety of historical forms of Taoism represents a concealed unity, or that everything commonly classified under the broad rubric of Taoism partakes of this unity. It would be just as inaccurate to represent all forms of Taoism as part of a whole as it would be to represent Taoism as a welter of individual cults. There are several reasons for variety in Taoism: historical responses to different social and cultural situations, specialization in particular branches of Taoist arts and sciences, and encapsulation of spin-offs based on obsession with specific techniques.

One of the tasks taken up by the Complete Reality movement was to distinguish the source from the outgrowths and establish a practical basis for understanding and reliving the essence of Taoism. From this standpoint the Complete Reality adepts were able to uncover the place and function of all the different grades of authentic and spurious Taoism, revealing the inner workings of Taoism with unprecedented clarity and reestablishing the experience held to link all enlightened people of all times.

Ironically, one of the most comprehensive descriptions of Taoism as it is understood in advanced Taoist circles can be found in a Buddhist text, the *Avatamsaka-sutra* or *Flower Ornament Scripture*, which is held to contain the totality of all religion:

*The various methods and techniques of the enlightened adapt to worldly
conditions in order to liberate people. The enlightened provoke deep faith
by being in the world yet unaffected by it, just as the lotus grows in water yet
water does not adhere to the lotus.*

*With extraordinary thoughts and profound talent, as cultural leaders,
like magicians the enlightened manifest all the various arts and crafts of the
world, like song and dance, and conversation admired by the people.*

*Some become grandees, city elders; some become merchants, caravan
leaders. Some become physicians and scientists, some become kings and of-
ficials.**

This Buddhist scripture uses the same idea to explain one of the most
ancient associations of Taoism, that of the originators of civilization itself as people of higher knowledge attained through extradimensional
awareness: "If they see a world just come into being, where the people do
not yet have the tools for livelihood, the enlightened become craftsmen
and teach them various skills." From this point of view, the Taoist vision
of ancient Chinese culture heroes as esoteric adepts is more than a pleasant myth. In essence it means that Taoism is not, as usually thought, a
product of Chinese civilization. Rather it is the other way about—
Chinese civilization was originally a product of Taoism in the sense that
like all successful original cultures it was initiated and guided by people
in contact with the Tao or universal law.

Extravagant as this idea may seem to moderns who conceive of ancient humans as semiconscious primitives who somehow slowly
evolved by fits and starts into civilized nations, it nevertheless explains
something about the concentration of knowledge for which neither
written history nor conventional psychology can account. It also means
that the fundamental nature and mission of Taoism is not Chinese; again,
as the *Flower Ornament Scripture* says, "All-sided goodness abides by reality, not in a country."†

---

*"Chief in Goodness," from Cleary, *The Flower Ornament Scripture*, vol. I (Boston: Shambhala Publications, 1984), pp. 330–67.
†"The Meditation of the Enlightening Being Universally Good," from *The Flower Ornament Scripture*, vol. I, pp. 176–81.

The earliest culture hero of China, one of the luminaries of the sacred Taoist sky, is Fu Xi (Fu Hsi), best known as the originator of the symbols of the ever-popular classic *Book of Changes*. Believed to have been a man of knowledge of very remote times, Fu Xi is said to have been the originator of animal husbandry and written symbols. Modern academics believe that the *Changes* signs were crude markers for use in divination, but Taoist tradition has it that special knowledge was put into the signs and extracted by civilizers of later eras of prehistory. Fu Xi is said to have obtained his knowledge by scientific study of natural, divine, and human phenomena, and the tradition of including these elements as parts of a curriculum of higher studies has been maintained by Taoists ever since.

Fu Xi is classically thought of as the first of the Three August Ones, the founders of Chinese civilization. After Fu Xi was Shennong, the August One who taught the people agriculture and horticulture, while his wife taught them sericulture. The third of the August Ones was Huang Di, popularly called the Yellow Emperor, who arose among people of a different race that had come into contact with the people descended from Fu Xi and Shennong.

The character of Huang Di is rather different from those of Fu Xi and Shennong, and he plays a larger part in Taoist lore. Before turning to this figure, however, there are two women of remote antiquity who made monumental contributions to early Chinese civilization and deserve special mention, one known as Guonu and one known commonly as the Golden Mother or Queen Mother of the West.

Guonu is a very mysterious figure whose great importance seems to relate to a crisis period accompanying the end of an immemorial migration. According to legend, she is most famous for having remedied serious dislocations in the psychic makeup of her people; from this operation is said to have emerged the science of the five elements or five forces, shadows of which pervade most of later Chinese thought. Guonu is supposed to have established the idea of homeland and to have introduced countermeasures to the savage rapacity that had emerged through the breakdown of the intuitive order of the human mind.

In contrast to Guonu as a figure of remote prehistory, the Queen

Mother of the West is thought of as prehistorical, as living in the historical past, and as existing in the eternal present. The Queen Mother of the West is sometimes considered the first woman of civilized times to attain permanent consciousness, figuratively represented as immortality. She is of the premier rank in the sacred Taoist sky and is in charge of all female seers, both those who leave the world and those who remain in the world. The Queen Mother herself is believed to live in the Kunlun Mountains, abode of immortals living on earth and fabled repository of esoteric knowledge. There are many fascinating stories of the doings of the Queen Mother of the West and her wards in the interstices of history.

The figure of Huang Di, the Yellow Emperor, stands like a colossus on the border of prehistory. Unlike the earliest civilizers, Huang Di is represented as having assumed his political leadership while still in ignorance of higher laws. His enlightenment came about not only through his own efforts and divine inspiration, but through his studies with other human teachers. Among the most famous of Huang Di's teachers were the Original Woman of the Nine Heavens, who taught him magical arts of warfare and mastery of occult energies, which he used to overcome violent tribes; the Plain Woman, who taught him the science of sexual energetics; the Man at the Crossroads, who taught him internal medicine; and the Master of Expanded Development, who taught him the art of immortality.

Huang Di is of such importance in Taoist tradition that Taoism is sometimes even named after him. To him is attributed one of the greatest of Taoist texts, perhaps the first to be put into words, the *Yin Convergence Classic*. The earliest commentary on this text is said to have been written prior to 1100 BC, with many more to come over the next two millennia. Typical of Taoist texts, this classic has widely varying interpretations, both martial and cultural. It is very highly valued among Taoists of the Complete Reality tradition (who typically give it a purely spiritual interpretation) and is placed in the first rank of Taoist literature by the founder of the Southern School of Complete Reality in his own latter-day classic *Understanding Reality*,* in turn one of the main sourcebooks for *The Book of Balance and Harmony*.

*See Cleary, *Understanding Reality* (Honolulu: University of Hawaii Press, 1987), II, 58.

There are also a number of key stories about the Yellow Emperor in popular Taoist literature—the classic *Liezi*, for example, *The Book of Master Lie*—which emphasize the Taoist view of politics as a lower art than self-cultivation. The fact that throughout history Taoists have taken diverse positions with regard to political matters—now passive, now aggressive, now aloof, now involved—should not obscure the central belief that there is a certain balance between higher and lower affairs that should be maintained for optimum efficiency of the human experience and must be restored when lost.

The importance of personal cultivation before assumption of leadership in society is also emphasized in the short classic *Guangchengzi* (*Book of the Master of Expanded Development*), represented as the teaching given by this illuminate to the Yellow Emperor after nearly two decades of the emperor's earthly rule had passed but the physical, social, and psychological condition of his person and his realm was deteriorating unnaturally. This establishment of priorities then serves as an introduction to the science of physical longevity and spiritual immortality, the former being the result of the practices conducive to the latter.

This teaching is put in terms consistent with basic meditation practices found throughout Taoism and Buddhism: "The essence of the ultimate Tao is mysterious and obscure; the furthest reach of the supreme Way is dark and silent. Without looking or listening, embrace spirit to become quiet, and the body will correct itself. Be quiet, be clear; don't strain your body, don't upset your vitality, and you can live long. When eyes see nothing, ears hear nothing, and mind knows nothing, your spirit will preserve your body, and your body will live long. Be careful of what is inside you, shut out what is outside you; being a busybody will destroy you. . . . I preserve unity, thus to participate in its harmony. . . . I share the lights of the sun and moon, I share the eternity of heaven and earth."

A commentary on the *Guangchengzi* by the illustrious poet, statesman, and mystic Su Shi notes the statement of another ancient text that the Master of Expanded Development, teacher of the Yellow Emperor, had mastered the *I Ching* hexagrams DIFFICULTY and DARKNESS.

These two hexagrams are traditionally used in Complete Reality Taoism to represent practice, and the claim that this adept of remote antiquity had mastered them illustrates another common Taoist idea that is not shared by secular scholars—the idea that the full elaborations of the hexagrams antedate the kings who wrote the words to the *I Ching* and in fact derive from the original signs of Fu Xi himself. This claim is made, not on the basis of the archaeological or historical record, but on the basis of the signs themselves.

In any case, there is no doubt that the *I Ching*, the *Book of Changes*, has been regarded as a basic text by Taoists since ancient times. Early Confucian commentaries were at some point incorporated into the received text of the *I Ching*, and Confucians prized it for the sociological and political lessons they found there. Even today there are those who believe that the *I Ching* is a Confucian rather than a Taoist text. Taoists, however, regard pristine Confucianism as a branch of Taoism and have been able to use the *I Ching* for their inner teachings without contradicting the exoteric "Confucian" usage.

There are numerous programs for Taoist use of the *I Ching*, ranging from the "sudden enlightenment" understanding of the "uncharted" or "unmarked" signless process of "nondoing" to the "gradual enlightenment" understanding of the entire text as a representation of the total process of "doing," or structured praxis. Among the most distinguished contributions of esoteric Taoism to *I Ching* learning is the *I Ching* mandalas,* the body of diagrams and arcana attributed to Taoist methodologists (*fangshi*) of the Han dynasty (206 BC–AD 219) that became public during the Song dynasty (960–1278). These mandalas are said to contain both the practical meditative lore behind the *I Ching* and structured programs for reading the text.

The original written text of the *I Ching*, articulating readings of the meanings of the ancient signs of Fu Xi, is traditionally ascribed to King Wen and the Duke of Zhou, two ancient leaders who founded the Zhou dynasty shortly before the beginning of the first millennium BC. The

---

*See Cleary, *I Ching Mandalas* (Boston: Shambhala Publications, 1989).

Zhou dynasty is noted for its transition from the slave economy of the preceding Shang dynasty (1766–1122 BC) to a feudal economy.

Shang barbarism, characterized by state-sponsored superstition, dehumanization of common classes, and sheer lust for possessions, to the Taoist mind represented a deterioration of the human condition typical of societies where myth has deposed true science and material force has replaced spiritual power. The mind of the Zhou dynasty, by contrast, ushered in by revelation of the meaning of the ancient lore in the *I Ching*, is more humanistic and approaches nature and spirit with respect rather than fear.

The Zhou dynasty lasted in name for some eight hundred years, but after the first few centuries the political reality had changed drastically. The various feudal states under the Zhou suzerainty lost the ritual and ethical cohesion of earlier times; gradually at first, later at a raging pace, they began to vie with one another for preeminence, eventually ushering in a long period of warring states.

The degeneration of the Zhou order encouraged the flowering of public and semipublic philosophical and spiritual schools in the middle of the first millennium BC. With this general period are associated such illustrious names as Confucius, the great educator, and Li Er, the "ancient master" Lao-tzu or Laozi, believed to have transmitted a famous collection of key Taoist lore. Both of these figures are greatly honored by Taoists, and the remains of their teachings—Confucius' *Analects* and Li Er's *The Way and Its Power*—are perhaps the two most popular and influential books in the mental history of China.

Somewhat later came the great Confucian Mencius and the great Taoist Zhuangzi, who also left books that became extremely popular classics. Both Confucius and Mencius are claimed by Taoist tradition, but the latter's connection to the Taoist stream is often considered to be more obvious. The Song dynasty neo-Confucians of the School of Inner Design, who revived the inner element of original Confucianism, especially emphasize this aspect of Mencius.

Mencius dealt with political and ethical questions in a manner typical of the sociological bent of the Confucian specialization within Taoism.

In contrast to the manifest sobriety of Mencius, Zhuangzi took the vehicle of humor and the flight of the imagination in order to convey certain sensibilities to the people of his time, an age of rapidly growing militarism. It may not be too much to say, in fact, that Zhuangzi and his school originated fiction as an overt operation in Chinese literature; and throughout the ages since, the most inspired and sophisticated novelists and poets have all steeped their minds in Taoism.

Other outstanding figures of approximately the same era who are also claimed by unitarian Taoist tradition are Mozi, the Tattooed One, and Master Sun the Martialist. The Tattooed One was at once a spiritualist and an engineer who preached universal love, leveling of society through elimination of luxurious living among the upper classes, and the connection of conscience to divine will. His response to the militarism of his time was to organize a group of humanitarian warriors and military engineers who traveled about constantly to defend the weak against the depredations of the strong. Sun the Martialist, on the other hand, taught the anatomy of conflict, both material and psychological, geared toward obviating the necessity for actual violence and minimizing it when it does occur.*

The final dissolution of the Zhou dynasty in both name and reality took place at the hands of the First Emperor of Qin (Ch'in). One of the most controversial figures in Chinese history, the First Emperor is also linked by some to the celestial court of Taoist inner government through his tutelage under legalist Confucian and immortalist Taoist teachers. The legalist Confucians believed that since human rule had become insufficient due to population growth and gradual loss of pristine conscience and morale, the rule of law was now needed to supersede individual will. Under the rule of the First Emperor, China was unified with respect to its writing system, its laws, and its weights and measures. Communications were opened, travel and commerce were encouraged. Private ownership and alienation of land by commoners was legalized, abolishing the ancient feudal system of the Zhou.

The short but momentous Qin dynasty was superseded by the Han.

*See Cleary, *The Art of War* (Boston: Shambhala Publications, 1988).

Although Western and Middle Eastern nations derive their names for China from the Qin dynasty, China's majority race derives its name for itself from this Han dynasty, so strong is the stamp of its four-century-long rule on the mind of Chinese history. The Han dynasty lasted from 206 BC to AD 9, when it was briefly overthrown by reformers in favor of the Xin or "New" dynasty, but reasserted itself in AD 25 to last until 229. The early Han dynasty is often called the Former Han, while the continuation is known as the Latter Han. An early emperor of the Former Han was persuaded by a certain scholar to authorize the creation of an intellectual orthodoxy—a combination of all the major trends of thought under the rubric of Confucianism. This enterprise led to the creation of state organs for the maintenance of this orthodoxy, which in turn produced a larger educated class than had ever before existed.

A typical member of this educated class might concentrate on one or another branch of Chinese science at different times, largely depending on one's time of life. If employed by the state as an administrative official or a professor, one would appear to be a Confucian in the daytime, but when at home at night or unemployed or in retirement one would more likely be a Taoist of one sort or another. Many women of the noble families, for example, excluded from public life yet free from the necessity of doing housework and taking care of children personally, became outstanding adepts in Taoist immortalism.

After the establishment of the Han dynasty and the ending of the early wars and conquests, a number of Han emperors took a Taoist approach to government, allowing the people to recuperate their energy and develop themselves with a minimum of interference. This Taoist influence added strength to the dynasty itself, yet paradoxically it produced an undertow of new thought and knowledge that the mental structure of the Han dynasty ultimately could not encompass. Such was the eventual deterioration of the Latter Han that hundreds of orthodox Confucian college students were openly massacred for expressing their desire to return to the way of Confucius and Mencius.

As early as Zhuang Zhou (Zhuangzi) the famous Taoist master of the fourth to third centuries BC to whom is attributed the classic *Chuang-tzu*, one finds evidence of the fragmentation of ancient Taoist knowledge and practice. Many of the "real people," whom Taoists believe guide the true progress of humankind, are said to have gone into hiding during the prolonged warfare that ravaged the ancient homeland of the Yellow Emperor. In the absence of general knowledge of the realities of Taoism the fragmentation of Taoism in both its social and esoteric forms continued apace through the Han dynasty. The arcane *Triplex Unity*, written shortly after the demise of the Han to elaborate on a laconic text of the late Han, devotes an entire chapter to specific obsessions leading misguided Taoists into aberration.

There was, nevertheless, a wider stream of Taoism running through the Han dynasty, evidenced by the great Taoist classic *Huainanzi* of the early Former Han and its early exegetical works of the Latter Han. Compiled by a king of the Liu family, the imperial clan of the Han dynasty, in concert with a small circle of Taoist practitioners and a group of Confucian practitioners, *Huainanzi*, or *Masters of Huainan*, ranges over many subjects from politics to spiritual alchemy. The *Huainanzi* book approaches the problem of Taoism's degeneration by unifying its scattered lore, and such is its scope that it is said the depths of Taoism cannot be known without delving into the *Huainanzi*. There is much in this book, however, that is heavily veiled, a compromise between the need for a more comprehensive presentation than one-track cults and the need for security in matters of power.

The end of the Han dynasty was heralded by massive uprisings, some of which were Taoist inspired. During the Latter Han, a spiritual and social movement called the Way of Great Peace appears to have stirred into action; somewhat later the Way of the Celestial Teachers appeared, as charismatics using their magical gifts for healing and social harmonization gained political independence for their settlements. The radical insurgency ending the Han dynasty tended to sort out different powers in both the exoteric and esoteric worlds. At times, esoteric kingdoms and magical freemasonries became semipublic, the more easily accepted for the disturbances caused by smaller nomadic and seminomadic nations taking over political control in what had for centuries been Han territory.

xvii

With the end of the Han dynasty, the barriers that had been set up by the self-reflection of the Han mind lowered sufficiently to allow the expression of both the fruits and the bewilderments of centuries of occult studies. For the next few centuries Buddhism flooded into China, and Confucians, Taoists, and Buddhists all worked together, sometimes by argument, sometimes by cooperation, to produce whole new skies of Chinese thought.

Three great Taoist texts mark the transition period ushering in this era, when Buddhism was still a foreign cult: the *Triplex Unity*, the *Book of Master Lie*, and the *Book of the Simpleton*. The *Triplex Unity* is said to be the first public revelation of the inner meaning of the *I Ching*, or *Book of Changes*, but it is in many places so arcane itself that nearly a thousand years elapsed before it became widely appreciated. It is closely related to a simpler late Han dynasty work.

The *Book of Master Lie* (Liezi or Lieh-tzu) is a compilation of Taoist lore ranging from abstract descriptions of the origin of awareness, perception, and thought to colorful stories illustrating complex psychological processes and jokes explaining metaphysical truths. This classic is to this day one of the most popular sources of folk wisdom.

The *Book of the Simpleton*, written nearly a century after the end of the Han, is largely devoted to the many questions involved in the studies of immortalism, alchemy, and government. One of the interesting features of this text is that it emphasizes the original inclusion of Confucianism within Taoism six centuries after the pre-Han rift that left many Confucian occultists without direction, and six centuries before the recollection of unity that characterized the Song dynasty under the influence of Buddhist panhumanism.

The interaction of Buddhism with Taoism over the following centuries produced greatly expanded Taoist canons and rites, as Taoist churches organized mass meditations like those of the rapidly growing Buddhist churches. Many Buddhist texts that were unused by mainstream Chinese Buddhism in its mature years seem to have left their traces most clearly in this great body of "religious" Taoist literature. Nevertheless, this literature does not seem to be an imitation of the Buddhist lore so much as a reexperience of it in the native Taoist-Chinese cultural domain.

The religious or church Taoist canon is generally divided into three parts with four supplements, known as the Three Open Channels and Four Auxiliaries. The Three Open Channels are the Open Channel to Reality, the Open Channel to Mysteries, and the Open Channel to Spirits. The Four Auxiliaries are called Absolute Mystery, Absolute Peace, Absolute Purity, and Correct Unification.*

The Open Channel to Reality contains the so-called Supreme Purity scriptures, the Open Channel to Mysteries contains the so-called Spiritual Jewel scriptures, and the Open Channel to Spirits contains the so-called Three August Ones scriptures. According to old writings recapitulated in a famous Taoist encyclopedia, the open channel of communication with reality is pure spirituality, the open channel of communication with mysteries deals with the mysteries of creation and life, and the open channel of communication of spirits deals with the summoning and control of lesser forces.

In practical terms, the encyclopedist notes that the open channel of communication with reality becomes accessible through "the high energy of whole clarity, absolutely unmaterialized." The open channel of communication with mysteries becomes accessible through "the energy of highly fluid openness, aware wholeness not reifying or being possessive of anything." The open channel of communication with spirits becomes accessible through the "energy of highly fluid openness to original nothingness, reaching the hidden by profound abstraction and quieting of the senses."

Among the Four Auxiliaries, the section on Absolute Mystery is auxiliary to the Open Channel to Reality; it is based on the ancient Taoist classic called *The Way and Its Power* transmitted by the ancient master Li Er or Lao-tzu. The section on Absolute Peace is auxiliary to the Open Channel

---

*The idea of the open channel, according to a recapitulation of a Song dynasty Taoist encyclopedist, is associated with communication. The Chinese word that is used commonly means cavern or vault, but in Taoist lore these mystic caverns prove to contain skies even vaster than those in the ordinary world outside; they are also pictured as passages to worlds of vast skies and luxuriant earths.

to Mysteries; it is based on scriptures strongly oriented toward ethical reflections of Taoism in politics and society. The section on Absolute Purity is auxiliary to the Open Channel to Spirits; it deals with alchemy. The section on Correct Unification is auxiliary to all three Open Channels; it contains recapitulations of the old teachings of the Way of the Celestial Masters, a hospitaler freemasonry turned Taocracy that normally included spiritual, social, and magical practices in unison.

The disturbance and disunion of the centuries after the fall of the Han dynasty ended with the Sui and Tang dynasties. Like the first unifying imperial dynasty of the Qin, the Sui dynasty was meteoric and monumental, laying the foundation for the three centuries of the Tang dynasty, the third latter-day golden age of China. This period is marked by the development of the major schools of Chinese Buddhism and the further codification of church Taoism. It also seems to be the final age for the academic Confucian style of the Han and for the proliferation of Taoist chemistry books.

Political struggles among certain followers of Taoism, Confucianism, and Buddhism were fostered by some of the highly placed members of the ruling house of the Tang to minimize their various threats to the established order, but other followers of the three Ways were already beginning the great reunification that was to mark the following Song dynasty. Prepared by their own practices, Taoists had absorbed much of the inspiration of Buddhism between the Han and the Sui dynasties; now Buddhism, reemerging in forms adapted to China, used Taoist sciences in their own teachings, just as early translators and interpreters had used Taoist terms to render Buddhist scriptures into Chinese.

The Pure Land school is the first of the major schools to be distinguished in China. Its origins midway between the Han and Tang dynasties coincide with the early development of the Three Open Channels literature in Taoism, and its prayer, meditation, and visualization practices have much in common with religious Taoism. Throughout Chinese history, there has always been a close affinity between the idea of the Buddhist Pure Land and the sacred skies of the Taoists where the immortals dwell.

One of the early Buddhist Pure Land patriarchs was originally a student of Taoist immortalist alchemy, but he was won over to the immortality of the vision of the Buddha of Infinite Light. Half a millennium later, the Complete Reality Taoists said the alchemical literature of that time had been confused, misunderstood; now one of the Taoist patriarchs was originally an enlightened Chan Buddhist who came to Taoism for the recovered science of life.

After the Pure Land school, the next to distinguish itself was the Tiantai school, a vast and comprehensive teaching based in theory on the "crown jewel" of Buddhism, the Lotus Sutra. In practice it was based on the sutras of transcendent wisdom with the meditations of the school variously known as the School of the Middle Way, the School of Openness, or the School of Essence, based on the teachings of the Indian sage Nagarjuna on *sunyata* or emptiness. The Tiantai school has a theoretical place for all the manifestations of Taoism in the Lotus Sutra's teaching about universal compassion; it has a practical place in its meditation teachings, where Taoist medical science is adopted to cure illnesses that the practitioner is not advanced enough to heal metaphysically.

Three more major schools appeared in the early Tang dynasty. The Chan school, the precursor of Zen that traced its origins back to the turn of the fifth century, emerged into public view during the vigorous seventh century with large independent organizations that sent developed individuals out into communities all over China to harmonize enlightenment with local conditions. Chan Buddhism is well known for using basic Taoist meditation techniques in the attempt to experience communion with the Dharmakaya, or reality body, considered most fundamental to Buddhist enlightenment. Later, Complete Reality Taoism recovered these techniques from Chan Buddhists and used them with great effect in unlocking lost mysteries of Taoism. In turn, eventually Chan Buddhists regularly adopted Taoist knowledge of medicine and exercise, while Taoists for their part attribute some of their own lore to the Indian founder of Chan Buddhism in China.

The Huayan school also became prominent during the early Tang dynasty. Immense in scope and comprehensive as the Tiantai school,

Huayan Buddhism is based on the *Flower Ornament Scripture*; the teachings of Vijnanavada or the Buddhist School of Consciousness play an important part in the praxis. Both the theoretical and practical place of all sorts of Taoism in pan-Buddhist terms are represented in the *Flower Ornament Scripture*, while the Taoist idea of celestial government intervening on earth corresponds with the scripture's unifying theme of Universal Good in infinite manifestations.

The esoteric Zhenyan or Mantra school of Buddhism, which flourished briefly during the Tang dynasty, made extensive use of ritual, incantation, visualization, and other techniques close to those used by religious Taoists. There is reason to believe that pre-Tang esoteric Buddhism had found its way into Taoist circles during the formative centuries of religious Taoism, and there is no doubt that Central Asian esoteric Buddhism was again absorbed by some Taoists, notably those of the Southern School of Complete Reality.

In terms of thought and practice, Buddhism and Taoism were well prepared for the rediscovery of common ground that was to mark the Song dynasty following the Tang. Politically, the waxing and waning fortunes of the two religions during the Tang dynasty went from temporary installation of classical Taoist studies as an alternative route to civil service on a par with Confucianism, on the one hand, to persecution of Buddhism near the end of the dynasty with such severity that only the Chan and Pure Land schools survived. The Tang dynasty's political backlash against Buddhism, however, actually brought the three Ways closer together, as Confucianism and Taoism themselves were permanently altered by the Buddhist elements they included within their own praxes.

Within the context of Taoism, one of the greatest figures in the re-amalgamation of the three Ways was the immortal Lu Yan, also called Lu Dongbin ("Visitor of the Hollow") or Luzu ("Ancestor Lu"). Traditionally said to have been a man of the Tang dynasty, according to legend Lu was a Confucian scholar with an advanced degree who turned to Taoism after having met one of the ancient adepts. Lu's teacher, Zhongli Quan, is said to have been a man of the Tang dynasty, but it is also claimed that he had been a general during the Han dynasty who retired into the mountains to learn the secrets of immortality.

Zhongli Quan and Lu Yan are both included among the most familiar immortals in popular Chinese folklore, but it is the latter in particular who stands out in Taoist tradition. All sorts of texts are attributed to Lu Yan as one of the functionaries of the Taoist esoteric government, believed to reappear on earth from time to time and to be accessible to mortals through mediums or automatic writers. The works associated with Lu Yan cover an unusually wide range of Taoist lore, but their most general mark is the idea of the unity of the three Ways of Taoism, Buddhism, and Confucianism.

As "Ancestor Lu," Lu Yan is considered the ancestor of the Complete Reality school of Taoism, for his disciple Liu Cao was the teacher of Zhang Boduan (983–1082), founder of the Southern school, and both Lu and Liu were teachers of Wang Zhe (1113–1171), founder of the Northern school. While so much lore has been attributed to later appearances or communications of Lu Yan that it is at times difficult to extract the early form of his teaching, the case of his disciple Liu Cao is much simpler. There are a few works attributed to Liu, including *Song of the Ultimate Way*, giving a summary of his teaching in which the affinity with Chan Buddhism is clearly evident, prefiguring the essence of the Complete Reality movement in Taoism.

"The body of illumination lasts forever," writes Liu in his song, "empty yet not empty; the mirror of awareness contains the sky, accommodating all things." Using Buddhistic terminology, this song shows the characteristic Complete Reality understanding of immortalism on an essentially spiritual plane. Liu then follows with a classic prescription for attainment that is common to Chan Buddhism and ancient Taoism: "When the home is empty and peaceful, the spirit naturally stays there," referring in typical metaphor to the practice of inward silence ordinarily used to break the force of mundane conditioning. Liu also emphasizes the common Chan Buddhist practice of mindlessness, which in Taoist terms means freedom from the compulsions of the human mentality: "Respond to people without minding, and spiritual transformation will be swift. The mindless mind is the real mind; when movement and still-ness are both forgotten, that is dispassion."

This basic practice of inner silence and mindlessness figures promi-nently in certain kinds of Buddhist and Taoist lore, but like the "hollow" concept of older Taoism as an open channel to a vaster realm of experi-ence, it is considered a prelude to life beyond. Complete Reality Taoism emphasizes a quasi-duality—essence and life—within the Tao. In terms that would become standard in the school, Liu Cao writes, "Spirit is es-sence, energy is life; when spirit does not run outside, energy is naturally stable."

The unification of essence and life, or spirit and energy, is considered of utmost importance in Complete Reality Taoism; indeed, degenera-tion in both Buddhism and Taoism is commonly attributed to imbalance between spirit and energy practices. Liu writes, "Don't think holding your breath is a true exercise; even counting breaths and contemplating designs are not. Even if you have cast off external concerns, if you still have inner mental entanglements, what is the difference in either case? Just observe the baby in the womb—does it know how to make subcon-scious calculations? Unify your energy and make it flexible, and the spirit will be permanently stabilized. The true breath going and coming is nat-urally unhurried, an extended continuum traveling around, returning to original life. Then even though you do not draw on it, the spiritual spring spontaneously flows at all times."

The science of essence or spirit, which is common to Complete Real-ity Taoism and Chan Buddhism, is held to be utterly simple, accessible to everyone, and said to be possible to accomplish on one's own, though its path is not without characteristic pitfalls. The science of life or energy, on the other hand, has a great range of complexities, contains much that is kept secret, and requires the instruction of a teacher. Complete Reality literature contains no end of criticisms of infatuated practitioners of me-chanical regimens of mental and physical exercises—cultists generally characterized as being sidetracked in fragments of the science of life without the underlying science of essence.

In Liu Cao's *Song of the Ultimate Way* the balance of essence and life is maintained in a manner that came to be characteristic of Complete Reality Taoism, through what in alchemical terms is called pouring spirit and energy into each other. On the literary plane this is accomplished by a combination of images representing the use of energy leading into spirit and the effects of spirit emerging in the experience and use of energy.

"The great work takes thirty-six thousand microyears," the song continues, "in which are seasons of yin and yang." This statement refers to the idea of one year containing thirty-six thousand intervals of attention, in each of which are found the wax and wane of spirit and energy. This was considered the gestation period of the new human being. Continuous attention to the development of this mental "sacred embryo" throughout these thirty-six thousand intervals is taken to be the equivalent of the essence of thirty-six thousand years of normal awareness.

This process is supposed to produce a whole new being with a body based on energy rather than matter: "The steaming relaxes the passes and channels, changing the sinews and bones; everywhere is radiant light, penetrating everything. Parasites run out of the house of the earthly body." Liu then goes on to describe the climax and subsiding of the healing and renewing ecstasy followed by a return to essence, saying that you now find you have "just been on the terrace of awareness all along." In the aftermath of the rejuvenating experience, however, perception is opened: "In past years the clouds and fog obscured the Way; today, on meeting, the eye of the Way opens."

Liu continues with a characteristic reemphasis on cultivation of essence within life practice: "This is not done in a day and a night. This is our original reality, not a technique. In the dead of winter firm as iron and stone, fight back demons of mundanity, apply the power of insight. This all depends on being empty and aloof; return to purity and wholeness, and this is the clear calm land of Utopia."

The science of essence is associated with the Taoist practice of nondoing, as emphasized here and throughout Taoist literature, but the Complete Reality tradition emphasizes the ordinary need for effort to reach the state of nondoing, which in turn releases inconceivable potential. As Liu says, "In the beginning, what do you use to set up the foun-

dation? When you reach the point of nondoing, nothing is not done."
This effort does not necessarily mean formal exercise, but inner purifi-
cation. Liu says: "Images of objects in thoughts should be removed, vitality and spirit in dreams held fast. Not moving and yet not being still is
the great essential; not being square and yet not being round is the ultimate Way. When the original harmony is cultivated inwardly, you become real; when breathing is pursued outwardly, in the end you won't
understand."

True to their Chan-like rigor in matters of essence and spirit, in matters of life and energy as well, rather than fix upon gross manifestations
as did the cultists they criticized, the Complete Reality Taoists directed
their attention to the source, going from the old physiopsychology to a
new psychophysiology. Liu writes: "If the basic energy is not stabilized,
the spirit is insecure. Let insects eat away the roots of a tree, and the leaves
dry up. Stop talking about mucus, saliva, semen, and blood—when you
get to the basis and find out the original source, they are all the same.
When has this thing ever had a fixed location? It changes according to the
time, according to mind and ideas. In the body it becomes perspiration
when feeling heat, in the eyes it becomes tears when feeling sadness, in
the genitals it becomes semen when feeling attention, in the nose it becomes mucus when feeling cold. It flows all over, moistening the whole
body; ultimately it is nothing more than the spiritual water."

The term "spiritual water" is used symbolically for fundamental vitality and awareness; here the phrase echoes the idea that spirit and energy, the subtle forms of mind and body, are originally one. It is through
the practical expression of this identity that the spiritual healing of both
mind and body was accomplished by Taoist adepts. Liu says: "The spiritual water is hard to talk about; those who know it are rare. It sustains life
in everything, and derives from the true energy. If you just know how to
be peaceful and detached, without thought or worry, disciplined in con-
sumption and behavior, moderate in speech, then ambrosia of the finest
flavor will eliminate your hunger and thirst, and you will see the real El-
emental."

The two most famous disciples of Liu Cao were the nominal founders of the main branches of Complete Reality Taoism. In the eleventh century, the middle of the Song dynasty, Zhang Boduan (Chang Po-tuan) elaborated on the inner cultivation of the subtle body, hinted at in Liu Cao's song, and clarified the spiritual essence of alchemical tradition, laying the foundation of the Southern School of Complete Reality. His writings on alchemy, especially *Understanding Reality*,* are still classics of this Taoist genre.

The inner cultivation of the subtle body is the art of opening the "passes and channels," subtle organs of spirit/energy accumulation and transmission visualized in the body. In Complete Reality custom, this exercise is a quintessential, stripped-down version of certain Taoist techniques that had been practiced through the medium of elaborate rituals in older religious schools of Taoism. The system of the subtle passes and channels is akin to certain formulations of esoteric Buddhism, which is always noted for its affinity to the Southern School of Complete Reality Taoism.

Zhang's classic *Understanding Reality* still contained a great deal of crypticism to prevent certain meanings from falling into the wrong hands, so a considerable body of exegetical literature grew up around it, beginning among Zhang's own heirs. During the twelfth century a kindred but independent movement began with Liu Cao's other famous disciple, Wang Zhe. This, the Northern branch, deemphasized energetics and took up *Understanding Reality* with great interest from the point of view of their primary interest in essence and spirit.

The emphasis of the Southern school is conventionally said to approach essence through life, while that of the Northern school is said to approach life through essence. One explanation for this difference is that the Southern approach is for older people whose energy is depleted, while the Northern approach is for younger people who have an excess of energy. In either case, *Understanding Reality* has always been regarded as a classic by both branches of the Complete Reality school, and it is one of the main sources for *The Book of Balance and Harmony*.

*For other writings of Zhang Boduan, see Cleary, *The Inner Teachings of Taoism* (Boston: Shambhala Publications, 1986).

In the commentary on *Understanding Reality* by Shangyangzi, one of the great Yuan dynasty writers of the Northern school, there is a list of metaphors for the two ingredients of dual spiritual alchemy, useful for relating the various alchemical works on this plane. The original text says, "When the two things join, sense and essence merge," and Shangyangzi notes that these "two things" may be called heaven and earth, being and nonbeing, sense and essence, fire and water, sun and moon, man and woman, dragon and tiger, lead and mercury, opening and subtlety, mystery and female, higher earth and lower earth, raven and rabbit, vitality and energy, turtle and snake, other and self, mind and body, metal and wood, host and guest, floating and sinking, hard and soft, lyre and sword, yin and yang. Most of these terms are used in *The Book of Balance and Harmony*, providing keys to understanding its alchemical teachings.

Generally speaking, *The Book of Balance and Harmony* follows *Understanding Reality* in its lineage and sources: the ancient *Book of Changes* and its early commentaries; the perennial Taoist classic *The Way and Its Power* and associated texts; the transcendent wisdom teachings of Buddhism, especially as practiced in Chan Buddhism; the tradition of alchemical immortalism deriving from the classic *Triplex Unity* elucidation of the *Book of Changes* that was brought to its full flower in *Understanding Reality*; and certain parts of the early Confucian classics and traditions.

The Book of Balance and Harmony also follows the tradition of *Chuang-tzu*, *Triplex Unity*, and *Understanding Reality* in repudiating certain practices as quasi-Taoist aberrations. In this it goes even further than earlier texts in its inventory of practices as well as in its classifications. The author of *The Book of Balance and Harmony*, Li Daoqun, had studied with sixteen or more teachers and is said to have learned the final secret from a mysterious personage in Central Asia. He evidently was therefore broadly familiar with the range of Taoist and Taoistic teachings and practices current in his time, including those of the Great Way and Absolute One schools, two other Taoist movements that arose in the same era as the Complete Reality school.

The first section of the book, as compiled by one of Li's disciples, is devoted to fundamental principles. The unity of the three Ways—Buddhism, Confucianism, and Taoism—is affirmed in respect to the plane of the absolute, or complete awareness. Then the central theme of balance and harmony is introduced from the *Record of Rites*, one of the early manuals of Zhou dynasty civilization, and the *Scripture of Purity and Clarity*, a short popular text ascribed to Lao-tzu, identified with Li Er, the transmitter of *The Way and Its Power*. The text then turns to the basic postures of Taoist practice. The section concludes with an introduction to the theme of the two minds: the real mind (the mind of Tao) and the errant mind (the human mind). A famous expression from the *Documents*, another early Confucian classic, is used to introduce this idea here as elsewhere in Complete Reality literature: "The mind of Tao is subtle, the human mind is insecure." It is the purpose of Taoist praxis to bring the subtle mind of Tao from the vagueness of the subconscious to the forefront of awareness in order to stabilize the human mind and eliminate its insecurity.

The second section of the book consists of a series of statements guiding the reader through an abstract visualization of evolution. Evolution has a twin meaning. It refers to the natural growth, development, and wane of all beings and also to conscious evolution said to be accomplished by evading unnecessary conditioning and taking direct recourse to the source. The first kind of evolution is referred to as going along; the second kind is called going in reverse. These are fundamental concepts of complete Taoist praxis, and basic understandings of the key ideas of essence and life are accordingly introduced in this section.

The third section of the book is devoted to meditations on nature, events, and oneself through the principles of the *Book of Changes*. The pervasive themes of change, rhythm, poise, perception, and adaptation are established in the consciousness of the contemplator through a series of meditation themes. Here again the author connects the pristine Confucian work on the *Book of Changes* with the tradition of the *Scripture of Purity and Clarity* so highly prized in Complete Reality Taoism.

The fourth section of the book goes into the science of the "gold pill," the alchemy of vitality, energy, and spirit. This section is divided into two parts, one corresponding to the science of essence and the other to the science of life. The alchemy of life is called the outer medicine and deals with matters of the physical body—energy, health, and longevity. The alchemy of essence is called the inner medicine and deals with the metaphysical body. The combination of these practices is held to produce mental and physical refinement and, ultimately, transcendence of space and time in awareness.

The fifth section of the book takes up a central formulation of the Complete Reality school known as the "three fives." This formula, taken from the classic *Understanding Reality*, is based on the diagrammatic arcana of the *Book of Changes*. The term "three fives" is a codified reference to three central concepts: the three bases or fundamentals, the five elements or forces, and the one energy. The three bases or fundamentals—vitality, energy, and spirit—are also called the three treasures, or the medicinal ingredients of the gold pill, the elixir of immortality. The five elements or forces are essence and sense, spirit and vitality, and will. The compounding of these five elements is one of the major operations of spiritual alchemy. The one energy is the fundamental energy of the universe, the source of the differentiated elements and bases of the alchemical human. This "compounding" process is explained as the unification of mind, body, and will—a cornerstone of Taoist praxis supposed to produce what are commonly called "real humans."

The sixth and seventh sections of the book deal with the central issue of the "mysterious pass"—the critical initiatory experience by which Taoists transcend the ordinary world. In the Complete Reality practice of seeking and opening the mysterious pass is one of the strongest signs of Chan Buddhist affinity within this school of Taoism. Other schools place the mysterious pass at various locations in the body or head, but Complete Reality purists insist there is no such location. Rather, in the opening of the metaphysical mysterious pass the Taoists of the Complete Reality schools found an experience of overwhelming importance that changed their outlook on the many yogic techniques in common practice.

The eighth, ninth, and tenth sections of the book present a compendium of practices in a hierarchic arrangement. In Complete Reality Taoism it is commonly said, particularly in reference to the mysterious pass, that there are thirty-six hundred practices, none of which is directly connected to the ultimate enlightenment. This book mentions many exercises and classifies them according to their effect, showing how the same terminology has different meanings according to the system of interpretation. These sections refer to the teachings of many unnamed sects. The scheme of categorization into lower, middle, and higher teachings is common to Buddhism and religious Taoism; the highest grade of practice in this scheme, presented in the tenth section, is little different from Chan Buddhism.

The eleventh, twelfth, and thirteenth sections consist of questions and answers. The eleventh section, on the underlying unity of Taoism, Confucianism, and Buddhism, uses the metaphysics of the *Book of Changes*, certain key passages from early Confucian classics, and some of the basic lore of Chan Buddhism to establish the esoteric connection among the three Ways. The twelfth section explains the practice symbolized by the alchemy of the gold pill in the teachings of the *Book of Changes*, *The Way and Its Power*, and *Understanding Reality*. The thirteenth section, focusing on alchemy, defines a number of important terms commonly used in alchemical texts.

The fourteenth and fifteenth sections present synopses of live teachings from the school of the author. These are teachings on the refinement of vitality, energy, and spirit, using practice based on the *Book of Changes* and *The Way and Its Power*.

The sixteenth section consists of two short discourses. The first concerns the subject of essence and life, the two basic facets of Taoist science, emphasizing the need for integration and completeness. The text notes that Buddhists of the time were fixated on essence whereas Taoists were fixated on life. This is a pattern to be seen again and again in the history of the confluence and divergence of these two Ways—a pattern which the Complete Reality school strove to eliminate in their praxis. The second discourse, on the symbolism of the signs in the *Book of Changes*, reconciles the direct formless practice, known as the highest alchemy that has no signs or lines, with the formal gradual practice traditionally encoded in the *I Ching*'s symbols. Here again the author follows the classic *Understanding Reality* and the pattern of Chan Buddhism.

The seventeenth section consists of two short discourses on basic meditation technique. These discourses are based on the teachings of *The Way and Its Power*, the *Scripture of Purity and Clarity*, and the *Book of Changes*.

The eighteenth and nineteenth sections contain songs and poems recapitulating the Complete Reality teachings. These works combine the vocabulary and imagery of ancient Taoism, alchemical Taoism, and Chan Buddhism. Poetry and song are among the best-known media of Taoist expression, and many works are written entirely in these forms.

The twentieth and final section, consisting of three essays on the three Ways of Buddhism, Taoism, and Confucianism, sums up the book with an inquiry into the essential theoretical and practical issues underlying the Ways. The main theme of these essays is transcendence of creation and change—the establishment of higher awareness beyond the vicissitudes of ordinary life and death.

THE
BOOK OF
BALANCE AND
HARMONY

I.

THE SOURCE MESSAGE OF THE MYSTIC SCHOOL

When you are calm and stable, careful of attention, the celestial design is always clear, open awareness is unobscured; then you have autonomy in action and can deal with whatever arises.

THE ABSOLUTE

The absolute is movement and stillness without beginning, yin and yang without beginning.

Buddhists call this complete awareness, Taoists call it the gold pill, Confucians call it the absolute. What is called the infinite absolute means the limit of the unlimited. Buddha called it "as is, immutable, ever clearly aware." The *I Ching* says, "tranquil and unperturbed, yet sensitive and effective." An alchemical text says, "Body and mind unstirring, subsequently there is yet an endless real potential." These all refer to the subtle root of the absolute.

So we know that what the three teachings of Buddhism, Taoism, and Confucianism esteem is calm stability. This is what a Confucian master called being based on calm. When the human mind is calm and stable, before it is affected by things, it is merged in the celestial design; this is the subtlety of the absolute. Once it is affected by things, then there is partiality; this is change of the absolute.

When you are calm and stable, careful of attention, the celestial design is always clear, open awareness is unobscured; then you have autonomy in action and can deal with whatever arises. With the maturation of practice of calm stability, one spontaneously arrives at this true restoration of the infinite, where the subtle responsive function of the absolute is clear and the design of the universe and all things is complete in oneself.

BALANCE AND HARMONY

Balance and harmony are the four directions centered on reality; in action all is balanced.

The *Record of Rites* says, "When emotions have not yet emerged, that is called balance; when they are active yet all in proportion, that is called harmony." Not having emerged means being careful of attention in the midst of calm stability; therefore it is called balance. Kept in attention yet immaterial, it is therefore called the root of the world. Proportion in action means being careful of what is manifested in action; therefore it is called harmony. Balanced in all actions, it is called arrival at the Way for the world.

Truly if one can be balanced and harmonious in oneself, then the being which is fundamentally so is clear and aware, awake in quietude, accurate in action; thus one can respond to the endless changes in the world.

Lao-tzu said, "If people can be clear and calm, heaven and earth will come to them." This means the same thing as the saying, "Effect balance and harmony, and heaven and earth are in place, myriad beings grow."

Balance and harmony are the subtle functions of sensitive efficiency, the essential workings of response to change, the totality of the cyclic movement and stillness of the flow of production and growth spoken of in the *I Ching*.

ALLOWING AND FOLLOWING

Allow the body to be tranquil, the mind to be clear, society to be integrated, events to be spontaneous. Then body, mind, society, and events follow the order, way, time, and design of nature, in responding to people, things, changes, and opportunities.

Body, mind, society, and events are called the four conditions. All worldly people make these into entangling bonds; only those who allow and follow can deal with them. Always dealing with them, yet always calm, one is no longer entangled.

What is allowing? It means allowing the body to be tranquil, allowing the mind to be clear, allowing society to be integrated, allowing events to be spontaneous. What is following? It means following the order of nature, following the way of nature, following the timing of nature, following the design of nature.

When the body follows the order of nature, one can therefore respond to people. When the mind follows the way of nature, one can therefore respond to things. When society follows the timing of nature, it is therefore possible to respond to change. When events follow the design of nature, it is therefore possible to respond to opportunities.

When one can allow, can follow, and can respond, then one is free and clear in the midst of the four conditions. Those who see this way are always responsive yet always calm, always clear, and always pure.

SHINING AND WANDERING

The shining mind is always calm; in action, it responds to myriad changes. Even when active, it is essentially always calm.

The wandering mind is always stirring; in quietude it produces myriad thoughts. Even when quiet, it is basically always astir.

Of old it has been said, always extinguish the stirring mind, don't extinguish the shining mind. The unstirring mind is the shining mind; the mind which does not stop is the wandering mind.

The shining mind is the mind of Tao, the wandering mind is the human mind. When it is said that the mind of Tao is vague, this means it is subtle and difficult to see. When it is said that the human mind is in peril, this means it is insecure and uneasy.

Even in the human mind there is the mind of Tao; even in the mind of

5

Tao there is the human mind. It is a matter of persistently keeping centered and balanced in activity and stillness, so that the shining mind is always present and the wandering mind does not stir. Then what was insecure will become peaceful, and what was vague will become clear.

At this point, the errant mind comes back, and the error-free Tao is accomplished. This is what the *I Ching* calls "coming back to see the heart of heaven and earth."

II.

STATEMENTS

*Forms all contribute to one another, beings are immanent in one an-
other; thus evolution and development go on without end.*

The Tao is basically utterly open. Utter openness has no substance. It
ends in endlessness, begins in beginninglessness.

When openness culminates, it transforms into spirit; spirit changes to
produce energy; energy masses into form—the one divides into two.

With duality, there is sensing: with sensing there is pairing of yin and
yang in mutual interaction. The creative and the receptive establish their
positions, movement and stillness alternate unceasingly; creativity, receptivity, vitality, and spirit interdepend, the active and passive take over
from one another. At this point, creativity, receptivity, desire, awareness, movement, stillness, attraction, and accord connect with the operation of essence, sense, spirit, vitality, and will, so that there is consis-
tency, establishing the seasons of the life cycle.

A harmonious process of distillation sustains origination and production: in heaven, it distributes the myriad forms; on earth, it nurtures all
living beings.

Forms all contribute to one another, beings are immanent in one another; thus evolution and development go on without end.

Everything in the world arises in being; being arises in nonbeing. Being and nonbeing interpenetrate, concealing and revealing each other in mutual interdependence.

Getting to the source of their beginning, we find all existents are based on energy. Discerning their end, we find all beings convert to form.

Thus we know that all beings are basically one form and one energy. Form and energy are basically one spirit. Spirit is basically utter openness. The Tao is basically ultimate nonbeing. Change is therein.

The position of heaven is above, the position of earth is below. Humans and other beings abide in the middle, spontaneously fluxing and evolving. Energy is therein.

Heaven and earth are the greatest of beings; humans are the most intelligent of animals. Heaven and humans are one; the universe is in their hands, myriad developments arise in their bodies. Transformation is therein.

The consummation of humanity is to establish life in the center of heaven and earth, to make essence of the endowment of open awareness. Establishing essence and life, spirit is therein.

Life is connected to energy; essence is connected to spirit. Plunge the spirit into the mind, gather energy in the body. The Tao is therein.

The enlightened make their energy and spirit complete. Through repeated harmonization they naturally become real.

The real within the real, the mysterious within the mysterious, the insubstantial producing substantiality—this is called the embryonic immortal.

If you want to reach the Tao, whence does it proceed? Be calm, be open, and there is hope of embryonic immortality.

When open, there is no obstruction; when calm, there is no desire. When openness is complete and calmness profound, observe the process of nature and know its cycles.

Let action proceed from calm, be filled by maintaining openness. These two principles are complementary; spirit and Tao are together.

The Tao is the host of the spirit, the spirit is the host of energy, energy is the host of the body, the body is the host of impulse. When there is no impulsiveness, the body rests; when the body rests, energy rests; when energy rests, spirit rests; when spirit rests, it does not dwell on anything—this is abiding without abode.

When the jewel of life is crystallized and the pearl of essence is bright, the original spirit is aware and the embryonic immortal is complete; then the path of open spontaneity is finished. How great is the spirit, the basis of transformation and evolution.

III.

SECRET MEANINGS

To master change, nothing is more important than to know the time;
to know the time, nothing is more important than to understand in-
ner design; to understand inner design, nothing is more important
than open calm.

IMAGES OF CHANGE

Change that can change is not eternal Change, images that can be imagined are not the Great Image. Eternal Change does not change, the Great Image is imageless. Eternal Change is change before delineation; changing change is change after delineation.

Eternal Change unchanging is the body of the absolute; changeable change is the basis of creation. The Great Image is the beginning of movement and stillness; that which can be imagined is the mother of form and name.

What is ever quiescent is eternal Change; that which never ceases is changing change. What is ultimately open and bodyless is the Great Image; what appears according to events is what can be imagined.

There is no way to find out the beginning or determine the end of the eternal; it is what clearly exists uniquely throughout all time. The Great outwardly contains heaven and earth, inwardly fills the universe; it is what pervades all worlds, profoundly still and perfectly complete.

Because eternal Change does not change, it can encompass the endless changes that take place in the world. Because the Great Image is image-less, it can describe the endless phenomena that occur in the world. Change and Image are the basis of the Tao.

ETERNITY AND CHANGE

Eternal Change does not change; changing change is not eternal. Because the eternal does not change, it can adapt to change; because the changing is not eternal, it can embody eternity. Never changing is the eternity of Change; the transiency of movement and stillness is the change of change.

Being invariably independent attains the eternal; going everywhere indefatigably masters the changing. Without knowing the eternal, one cannot master change; without mastering change, one cannot know the eternal. Eternity and Change are the basis of transformation.

SUBSTANCE AND FUNCTION

Eternity is the substance of Change, change is the function of Change. What never changes is the substance of Change; what changes with time is the function of Change.

Freedom from cogitation and contrivance is the substance of Change; sensitive adaptation is the function of Change. Knowing the function, one can find out the substance; preserving the substance, one can sharpen the function.

Sages gaze above and examine below, search afar and apprehend the near, to realize the substance; developed people advance in quality, accomplish works, carry out tasks, and create tools, based on the function.

Investigating truth, fulfilling human nature, taking pleasure in the celestial, knowing the meaning of life, cultivating harmony and peace, and arranging the social order are all within Change. Preserving the substance of Change is the way to know the eternal; sharpening the function of Change is the way to master adaptation.

MOVEMENT AND STILLNESS

The alternation of the firm and the yielding is the movement and stillness of Change. The rise and descent of yin and yang is the movement and stillness of energy. The coming and going of energy is the movement and stillness of things. Rising and retiring by day and night is the movement and stillness of the body.

The advancement and retirement of the individual, the arising and disappearing of thoughts, the fortune and misfortune of the world, the success and failure of affairs—all are alternations of movement and stillness. By observing their movement and stillness, the changes of events and the conditions of beings can be seen.

When there is attention in stillness, there is perceptivity in action. When there is autonomy in stillness, action can be decisive. When there is certitude in stillness, actions are auspicious. Stillness is the foundation of action, action is the potential of stillness. When action and stillness are always as they should be, one's path is illumined.

CONTRACTION AND EXPANSION

The coming and going of heat and cold is the contraction and expansion of a year. The coming and going of the sun and moon is the contraction and expansion of energy. The coming and going of past and present is the contraction and expansion of time.

The interdependence of being and nonbeing, difficulty and ease, long and short, high and low—all are the principle of contraction and expansion. If one knows the way of mutual influence of contraction and expansion, then one can comprehend endless benefits in the world.

WAXING AND WANING

Waxing is the beginning of waning; waning is the end of waxing. Waxing is the massing of energy; waning is the dissolution of matter. Growth and development is called waxing; returning to the root, submitting to destiny, is called waning.

Origin and growth are the waxing of change, fruition and consummation are the waning of change. Spring and summer are the waxing of the year, autumn and winter are the waning of the year. Youth and maturity are the waxing of the body, aging and death are the waning of the body. Going from nonbeing to being is the waxing of things, going from being to nonbeing is the waning of things.

Waxing is the cohort of life, waning is the cohort of death. Ever since the first division of positive and negative energies, there has never been a pattern of waning without waxing, and there has never been anything that waxed without waning. Those who realize this are clearly aware of truth.

SPIRIT AND POTENTIAL

What abides in the center is spirit, what emerges accurately is potential. What is silent and unstirring is spirit, what is sensitive and effective is potential. What appears and disappears unfathomably is spirit, what works responsively without convention is potential.

Potential is stored in the body, spirit is extended to myriad things. Potential foreshadows good and ill, spirit is ever fluid. Potential contains the qualities of creativity, development, fruition, and completion. Those who continually grow stronger are those who preserve this spirit. Those who comprehend heaven, earth, and humanity, functioning responsively without end, are those who use this potential.

KNOWLEDGE AND ACTION

Knowledge is profound knowledge of principle, action is powerful practice of the Way. Profound knowledge of principle knows without seeing, powerful practice of the Way accomplishes without striving.

To "know without going out the door, see the Way of Heaven with-

13

out looking out the window" is profound knowledge. To "grow ever stronger, adapting to all situations," is powerful practice.

To "be aware of disturbance before disturbance, be aware of danger before danger, be aware of destruction before destruction, be aware of calamity before calamity" is profound knowledge. "Preservation in the body without being burdened by the body, action in the mind without being used by the mind, working in the world without being affected by the world, carrying out tasks without being obstructed by tasks" is powerful practice.

By profound knowledge of principle one can change disturbance into order, change danger into safety, change destruction into survival, change calamity into fortune. By powerful practice of the Way, one can bring the body to the realm of longevity, bring the mind to the sphere of mystery, bring the world to great peace, bring tasks to great fulfillment. Who can reach this but those of great knowledge and great action?

UNDERSTANDING THE TIME

To master change, nothing is more important than to know the time; to know the time, nothing is more important than to understand inner design; to understand inner design, nothing is more important than open calm.

Openness means awareness, calm means clarity. When one is imbued with clear awareness, the celestial design is evident.

The transformations of heaven can be seen by observing change; the trends of the times in the world can be checked by observing images; the sincerity or falsehood of people can be discerned by observing concrete manifestations.

That which cleaves to concrete manifestations cannot but correspond to something; that which takes place in the material realm cannot be without distinguishing characteristics. When it is going to rain, there must be moisture in the air; when a mountain is going to crumble, the lower part must give way first; when people are going to render help or harm, their faces first change.

It is like knowing how windy it is from watching a bird's nest, knowing how much it has rained by seeing a puddle in a hole. Insects respond to the season, and when leaves fall we know it is autumn. It is also like a caravan using a pheasant's tail feather to forecast the weather: if it's going to remain clear the tail stands straight up; when it's going to rain the tail droops.

Even inanimate things are this predictable; people are even more so. Those who do not know the changes of the times have not yet clearly perceived their inner design.

CORRECTING ONESELF

To promote worthy qualities and accomplish works, nothing is more important than correcting oneself. Once the self is correct, everything is correct. Forms and names cannot stand but for correctness, tasks cannot succeed but for correctness.

All activities start from oneself. Therefore developmental work requires self-correction as a foundation. When one deals with people after having corrected oneself, then people too will become correct. When one manages affairs after having corrected oneself, affairs too become correct. When one responds to things after having corrected oneself, things too become correct.

Only a unified correctness in the world is able to master the myriad changes in the world. So we know that correcting oneself is the great function of developmental work, and the stairway into sagehood.

MEDITATION

Clearing the mind, dissolving preoccupations, purifying thought, forgetting feelings, minimizing self, lessening desire, seeing the basic, embracing the fundamental—this is meditation of the Transformative Way. When the mind is clear and freed of preoccupations, it is possible to fathom the design of reality; when thoughts are ended and feelings for-

15

gotten, it is possible to fathom the essence of reality. When selfishness and desire disappear, it is possible to arrive at the Tao; when one is plain and simple, pure and whole, it is possible to know the celestial.

SENSING AND RESPONSE

Comprehension in a state of quiescence, accomplishment without striving, knowing without seeing—this is the sensing and response of the Transformative Way. Comprehension in a state of quiescence can comprehend anything, accomplishment without striving can accomplish anything, knowing without seeing can know anything.

To sense and comprehend after action is not worthy of being called comprehension; to accomplish after striving is not worthy of being called accomplishment; to know after seeing is not worthy of being called knowing. These three are far from the way of sensing and response.

Indeed, to be able to do something before it exists, sense something before it becomes active, see something before it sprouts, are three abilities which develop interdependently. Then nothing is sensed but is comprehended, nothing is undertaken without response, nowhere does one go without benefit.

THREE KINDS OF I CHING

The three kinds of I Ching (Book of Changes) are that of the sages, that of heaven, and that of the mind. The Changes of heaven consist of the principles of transformation, the Changes of the sages consist of representations of transformation, and the Changes of mind consist of methods of transformation.

To view the Changes of the sages, it is important to understand the representations, for when the representations are clear you gain access to sagacity. To view the Changes of heaven, it is important to investigate principles, for when principles are investigated thoroughly you come to know the celestial. To view the Changes of mind, it is important to practice the Tao, for when the Tao is practiced you complete the mind.

If you do not read the Changes of the sages, you will not understand the Changes of heaven. If you do not understand the Changes of heaven, then you do not know the Changes of mind. If you do not know the Changes of mind, you cannot adequately master change. So we know the *I Ching*, The Changes, is a book for mastering change.

SOLVING CONFUSION

The waning and waxing of energy, the rise and fall of the times, the presence and absence of opportunity, the welfare and impasses of society— these are changes of heaven.

Auspicious and inauspicious signs, advantageous and disadvantageous elements, expressions of danger and ease, symbols of rectitude and obscurity—these are changes recorded by sages.

Impasses and achievements in life, advancement and withdrawal in status, success and failure in society, safety and danger in position—these are changes of mind.

If you have deep understanding of changes of heaven, you know the forces and momentum of the times. If you have deep understanding of the changes recorded by the sages, you know transformations and developments. If you have deep understanding of mental changes, you know essence and life.

One understands the changes recorded by sages through mental changes; one infers the changes in heaven by the changes recorded by sages. One looks into the mental changes by means of the celestial changes. One who realizes the single pervasive thread is called a person with will.

RESOLVING DOUBTS

Change and movement have their times; safety and danger are in oneself. Calamity and fortune, gain and loss, all start from oneself. Therefore those who master change are those who address themselves to the time. For those who address themselves to the time, even danger is safe; for those who master change, even disturbance is orderly.

Those who do not lose their control manage to get through even in an impasse; those who are not careful of their actions are befuddled even by wealth.

Those who conceal their illumination are unharmed even in the absence of understanding; those who rely on what they have dwell on great possession and are sure to suffer harm.

Those who can respond even while very distant have the same will; those who have nothing to do with each other though very near have conflicting intentions.

Those who are most weak yet can prevail have their underpinnings; those who are most strong yet have no excesses are imbued with the Tao.

Beneficial use of bad things solves difficulty; averting the gaze from evil people avoids resentment.

Those who are not constant in virtue have no tolerance; those who do not do their own tasks benefit no one.

Those who stand alone with pride in themselves accomplish nothing; those who are cautious and practice self-awareness gain fortune.

Others benefit those who benefit others; others help those who help others; others trust those who trust others; others are generous to those who are generous to others.

Those who beware of evil have no evil; those who beware of error have no error.

To those who beware of calamity, fortune will come; to those who slight fortune, calamity will come.

How can it be doubted that safety and danger are in oneself?

THE ACCOMPLISHMENT OF SAGES

The reason sages are sages is because of their application of the Changes. The means whereby application of the Changes produces accomplishment are openness and calm.

18

When open, one takes in all; when calm, one perceives all. When open, one can accept people; when calm, one can deal with events. When openness and calm are practiced for a long time, the awareness is clarified.

Openness is the image of heaven, calm is the image of earth. Spontaneous strengthening without cease is the openness of heaven, rich virtue supporting beings is the calm of earth. Empty vastness without bound is the openness of heaven; universal breadth without limit is the calm of earth.

The Tao of heaven and earth is this openness, this calm. When openness and calm are in oneself, then heaven and earth are in oneself. This is what is meant by the saying in Taoist scripture, "If people can always be clear and calm, all heaven and earth will come to them." Clarity is openness; openness and calm are the sages' accomplishment of spiritual qualities.

IV.

SECRETS OF THE GOLD PILL

The outer medicine is perfecting life, the inner medicine is perfecting essence. When the two medicines are complete, one is physically and mentally sublimated.

Stabilization of the Furnace

Supporting the universe, the great unknown;
Who gives it the name of the jade furnace?
Having gone through refinement herein,
One can leave nonbeing and enter being at will.

Setting Up the Cauldron

It is not nonbeing, not being, not in between;
Outside is void, inside is empty;
The decisive and energetic overturn it and see—
All along *that* has always been aglow.

Restored Elixir

It is originally clear, before history;
Obscurities are all due to fixation on illusory forms.
When you pick out the elixir,
It is round, open awareness.

Reverted Elixir

The Tao is originally uncontrived, patterned on nature;
Sages set up images, a sphere of temporary names.
In everyday life it is completely manifest,
But only when you break through do you know the primordial.

The Spoken Secret

Take the real consciousness out of the overlay of conditioning that obscures it, and use it to make awareness complete, restoring the celestial. With the pure creative root of life stabilized, the pearl of immaterial essence is perfect.

As a sensitive receiver, one preserves the celestial design; detached from objects, one accords with the highest meditation. When one knows how to go about gathering real knowledge, in three stages one activates the embryonic immortal.

When the mind does not stir, the energy is naturally stable. When the will does not waver, the spirit is naturally aware. When the body is not restless, the vitality is naturally stable.

Metaphors

Vitality in the body is yang within yin; refine vitality into energy. Energy in the mind is yin within yang; refine energy into spirit. The original spirit is formless; refine spirit into openness.

OUTER AND INNER MEDICINES

The outer medicine can be used to cure illness and prolong life. The inner medicine can be used to transcend being and enter into nonbeing.

Learning the Tao usually should start from the outer medicine; after that you come to know the inner medicine on your own. Advanced people who have already developed basic worthy qualities know it spontaneously, so they cultivate the inner medicine without cultivating the outer medicine.

The inner medicine involves no doing, but there is nothing it does not do; the outer medicine involves doing, and there is a way to do it.

The inner medicine has no form or substance, yet it really exists; the outer medicine has body and function, yet it really does not exist.

The outer medicine pertains to the physical body; the inner medicine pertains to the metaphysical body.

The outer medicine is perfecting life, the inner medicine is perfecting essence. When the two medicines are complete, one is physically and mentally sublimated.

THE OUTER MEDICINE

At the first pass, refining vitality into energy, it is first necessary to recognize the time when the primal vitality arises, and then quickly gather it.

At the middle pass, refining energy into spirit, one harmonizes the true breath, the inner pulse of life, so that it flows everywhere. From the bottom of the torso it flows backward up the spine to the head, where it mixes with the spirit. After that it descends to the solar plexus and enters the middle of the torso. When spirit and energy mate, a point of conscious energy appears in the center of the thorax.

At the upper pass, you refine spirit back into spacelike openness. Refining thought by mind is called seven-reversion; sense coming back to essence is called nine-restoration.

THE INNER MEDICINE

The inner medicine is essential for refining the spirit. When body and mind are both sublimated, merging in reality with the Tao takes place.

The inner medicine is the primordial point of true yang, the celestial. It is likened to the center line in the *I Ching* trigram HEAVEN ☰. When it mates with EARTH ☷, that forms WATER ☵. The center line represents true inner sense, which is firm and hence symbolized by metal, so it is also called metal in water. These are all names for ultimate vitality. When the ultimate vitality is stable, it reverts to generative energy.

The generative energy is the primordial, immaterial, unreified, real, unified, basic energy. It does not refer to oxygen in respiration. When the central line of HEAVEN ☰ has been injected into EARTH ☷, making WATER ☵, the central yin of EARTH is injected into HEAVEN, making FIRE ☲. The central yin of FIRE represents flexibility in consciousness; since it originates in EARTH, it is called mercury in sand.

The Tao produces one, one produces two, two produce three, three produce myriad beings: openness changes into spirit, spirit changes into energy, energy changes into vitality, vitality changes into form. This is called "going along."

Myriad beings are included in three (heaven, earth, beings), the three return to two (yin and yang), the two return to one: refine the ultimate vitality, and vitality turns to energy, energy turns to spirit. This is called "reversal."

Alchemical texts say "going along" produces people, "reversal" produces the elixir of immortality.

The three superior medicines are vitality, energy, and spirit. Their body is one, their functions are two. What is the body? It is the original great matter of the three bases. What are the functions? They are the inner and outer applications.

The inner medicines are primordial ultimate vitality, immaterial open energy, incorruptible fundamental spirit. The outer medicines are sexual vitality, the energy of breath, and the thinking spirit.

Refining Vitality into Energy

The first pass involves doing, taking from WATER ☵ to fill in FIRE ☲.

Taking to the Tao is seeking the mystery in the province of water, which represents vitality on the primal plane and desire on the temporal plane. Alchemical texts say, "When vitality arises, gather it at once; if you look afar, you can't taste it." Gathering is nongathering gathering; were there really something gathered, how could the central line in WATER, which represents something intangible, ever rise?

Vitality is an emanation of the primordial ultimate awareness: based on its action, the body comes to be; the ultimate vitality in the body is yang. "Gathering" means gathering this. This may be symbolically represented as HEAVEN ☰ being the primordial ultimate awareness; by one initial movement it mixes with EARTH ☷ and produces WATER ☵. This is a representation of the ultimate awareness emanating the fundamental vitality into the earthly plane.

The alchemical term "gathering lead" refers to gathering the inner sense of the vitality emanated by primal awareness. As this sense is firm and unequivocal, it is symbolized by metal and called "true lead." The experience of "gathering lead" is hard to describe. It is possible to understand much of it by pondering this statement from the *I Ching*: "THUNDER (movement) is in EARTH (stillness): RETURN. Kings of yore shut the gates on the winter solstice; the caravans did not travel, the lords did not inspect the regions." This means that the return of the movement of the primal vitality emerges from stillness; when it first arises, it is important to remain calmly attentive and not dissipate it by excitement or impulsiveness. The precise details of the process are secret, in that they must be passed on personally, according to individual circumstances.

Refining Energy into Spirit

In the middle pass, being and nonbeing interpenetrate; movement and stillness open and close.

Buddhists cultivate concentration in the chamber of FIRE, or conscious awareness. Taoist literature says, "Will stabilizes inner sense, inner sense stabilizes conscious knowing. When inner sense and conscious knowing submit to will, body and mind are tranquil." This statement is exhaustive. Once you find the true inner sense, there is no worry that consciousness will not be stabilized.

In refining energy, movement is essential: opening and closing, coming and going, rising and descending, without stopping. At first this is done consciously; later it becomes spontaneous. One exhalation and inhalation takes the place of the evolution of a year. This is the meaning of

Lao-tzu's saying, "The door of the mysterious female is called the root of heaven and earth. Continuously there as such, use of it is unforced."

If people focus their minds on the opening of the changes of movement and stillness, when movement emerges from stillness and when movement culminates and begins to revert to stillness, they will find the essentials of refining energy are all there.

Refining Spirit Back into Openness

In the upper pass there is no doing. When the work arrives at this stage, not a single word applies.

These three levels of work are one when accomplished. If you can perceive this with unified vision, then the great concern of Taoism, Buddhism, and Confucianism is done.

V.

EXPLANATION OF
THE THREE FIVES

Collecting body and mind is gathering medicine.

The alchemical classic *Understanding Reality*, by the adept Ziyang, says, "Those who understand the three words 'three, five, one' have always been truly rare. The east three plus the south two make five; the north one and the west four join; the production number of the center earth is five. When these three sets meet, they form an infant. The infant is unity imbued with true energy. In ten months the embryo is complete, entering the foundation of enlightenment."

These lines penetrate all the schools of philosophy, the alchemical classics, and the writings of the adepts. If you can see what is behind them, your study is done; if not, consider the following explanation.

"Three, five, one" refers to the three bases, the five forces, and one energy. The three bases are basic vitality, basic energy, and basic spirit. The five forces, or five elements, are essence, sense, spirit, vitality, and will.

The five forces are symbolized by wood, metal, fire, water, and earth; each of these is further associated with specific directions and numbers. "East three" stands for essence, "south two" stands for spirit. Essence and spirit relate to mind, so they are regarded as a family or set. "North one" stands for vitality, "west four" stands for sense. Vitality is the basis of the body, the body is the connector of sense. Vitality and sense relate to the body, so they are regarded as a set. The center, the number five, and the element earth all stand for will. Will is the director of the five forces; it has no partner and forms a set in itself.

So the five forces comprise three sets; the representative numbers of the members of each set add up to five, so these sets are called the three fives.

When the practitioner collects body, mind, and will, then the three bases and five forces naturally combine into one. This is what is meant when alchemical texts say, "Collecting body and mind is gathering medicine."

The essence of collecting body and mind is in openness and calm. Empty and open the mind, and spirit and essence join. Calm the body, and vitality and sense are still. When the will is greatly stabilized, the three bases—vitality, energy, and spirit—merge into one. This is called "the three flowers gathering on the peak," "the five energies returning to the source," and "the spiritual embryo congealing."

Sense uniting with essence is called "metal and wood joining." Vitality uniting with spirit is called "water and fire mixing." Great stabilization of will is called "completing the five forces."

Alchemical literature says, "Refining vitality into energy is the first pass—the body is not agitated. Refining energy into spirit is the middle pass—the mind is not agitated. Refining spirit back into openness is the upper pass—the will is not agitated."

The mind being undisturbed is what is meant by "east three plus south two make five." The body being undisturbed is what is meant by "north one and west four join." The will being undisturbed is what is meant by "the production number of center earth is five." Body, mind, and will uniting is "the three sets meet, and form an infant."

The meeting of the three sets means the three bases and five forces combine into one. Therefore it says that when these three sets meet they form an infant. The term infant means pure unity. Therefore it says the infant is unity imbued with true energy.

"In ten months the embryo is complete, entering the foundation of enlightenment." In three hundred days the two medicines in the embryo, conscious essence and true sense, in equal proportion, are refined and matured. This is the great accomplishment of transcending the ordinary and entering into sagehood, so it is called entering the foundation of enlightenment.

For those who see this, the task of spiritual alchemy is done, the great affair of spiritual immortality is completed. The various symbols and terms of alchemical texts do not refer to anything outside of body, mind, and will.

Body, mind, and will are called the three sets or three families. Vitality, energy, and spirit are called the three bases. Vitality, spirit, higher soul, lower soul, and will are called the five energies. The meeting of the three sets is called perfection of the embryo. Unification of the three bases is called completion of the elixir.

VI.

THE OPENING OF THE
MYSTERIOUS PASS

The body is like a puppet; the strings of the puppet are like the
mysterious pass. The person controlling the puppet is like the inner-
most self.

The opening of the mysterious pass is the most abstruse and most essential mechanism. It is not, as various practitioners of yoga say, in the forehead, or the navel, or the bladder, or the genitals, or between the kidneys
and navel, or between the kidneys and genitals. From head to heels, any
spot of the body you may focus on is not it. Yet it is not to be sought externally, apart from the body.

Therefore sages just used the word "center" to point out the opening
of the mysterious pass. This "center" is it. Let me give you a convenient
simile. When a puppet moves its hands and feet and gesticulates in a hundred ways, it is not that the puppet can move—it is moved by pulling
strings. And though it is a string device, it is the person controlling the
puppet who pulls the strings.

Do you know this person who controls the puppet? The puppet is
like the body, the strings are like the mysterious pass; the person controlling the puppet is like the innermost self. The movements of the

body are not done by the body; it is the mysterious pass that makes it move. But though it is the action of the mysterious pass, still it is the innermost self that activates the mysterious pass. If you can recognize this activating mechanism, without a doubt you can become a wizard.

VII.

THE GOLD-TESTING
STONE

*There are thirty-six hundred methods in Taoism; people each cling
to one and consider it fundamental. Who knows this opening of the
mysterious pass is not in the thirty-six hundred methods?*

The gold pill has open nonreification for its substance, clear calm for its
function; it is an unexcelled, subtle way to reality. Few people in the
world know this, few cultivate it; therefore sages, using their power of
skillful means, have opened up good avenues of introduction, setting up
terminology and imagery, writing alchemical treatises to guide students. If people who want to approach will familiarize themselves with
these writings, understand their principles, intuitively recognize them
and inwardly comprehend them, then when they apply them they will
at once transcend into the realm of reality.

Nevertheless, people of later times, failing to search out the inner design, have clung to the superficialities of the presentation, bringing in all
sorts of irrelevant issues, resulting in fragmentation of the Way into by-
ways and sidetracks, as many as thirty-six hundred of them. This is because they have not received transmission of the Way.

Even more mistaken are the ignorant shallow students of today who
arbitrarily write misinterpretations of the meaning of the classics of the

sages. This is certainly wrong, for those of the future will then be unable to distinguish the false and the true, no matter how hard they try. They are to be pitied.

It is because of these facts that I have composed this Gold-Testing Stone to distinguish the real from the spurious, so that students will not be confused but will settle all doubts and leap directly to the shore of the Tao.

An enlightened teacher has said, "There are thirty-six hundred methods in Taoism; people each cling to one and consider it fundamental. Who knows this opening of the mysterious pass is not in the thirty-six hundred methods?"

It seems to me that the teacher said this out of kindness. For anyone who can see in this way, the whole earth is gold. Otherwise, if you cannot see, you should make a test, so I have written it here.

VIII.

NINE GRADES
OF PRACTICES:
Sidetracks and Auxiliary
Methods

Some imagine the basic spirit going out and in through the top of the head. Some travel to the realms of wizards in dreams. Some silently pay court to the supreme god. Some consider oblivion to be entry into trance. Some consider counting breaths to be the firing process. Some imagine black and white energies of the heart and genitals merging.

THREE LOWER GRADES

I. LOWEST OF THE LOW: FALSE PATHS

These methods include seventy-two schools of sexual play, and in the vocabulary of these schools technical terms of alchemy are given sexual and quasi-sexual connotations. For example, some regard woman as the alchemical cauldron, and some use nine women as the "nine-cauldron." Some regard the first menses as medicine, some take menstrual fluid in general as the "ultimate treasure" and gather it to ingest it. Some take semen and menstrual blood as the bases of the great elixir; some have a virgin boy and girl copulate, and then gather their first sexual fluids as a tonic. There are over three hundred such practices. This is what is called "mud and water alchemy." These are paths of confusion, misleading paths.

2. MIDDLE-GRADE LOW PATHS: OUTSIDE PATHS

These methods include eighty-four other schools of sexual intercourse, with thirty-six modes of culling the female principle. There are also such practices as ingesting placenta, ingesting hormones distilled from urine, and ingesting one's own sexual fluid.

Here too technical terms are given biological associations: placenta is called the "violet energy cycle," ingesting one's own semen is called "return to the source," prevention of ejaculation during sexual intercourse is called "nonleaking," menstrual blood is called the "red pill."

Some people also feed a certain mineral compound to a woman so that she gives birth to a mass of flesh, and then they eat this as supreme medicine. Such fallacious techniques number over three hundred. They are outside paths, deviations from the Way.

3. UPPER-GRADE LOW: OUTSIDE PATHS

There are also over four hundred recipes for material alchemy to make potions to be ingested. These are outside paths.

These three low paths comprise over one thousand items. They are practiced by people who are lustful and greedy.

THREE MIDDLE GRADES

I. LOWER MIDDLE GRADE

Practices of the lower middle grade include abstention from grain, enduring cold, eating filth, eating the berries of the prickly ash, lying on ice with the back exposed, eating only once a day, and fasting completely. Being able to eat a lot may be considered a marvel, or drinking wine without becoming drunk may be considered miraculous. Some reduce their intake of food and call that "adding and subtracting." Some avoid flavoring and eat only bland foods. Some do not eat cooked food. Some drink wine and eat meat without concern for their health and claim to be uncontrived. Some perform various strange feats. These are the lowest of the middle grade.

2. MIDDLE MIDDLE GRADE

The middle middle grade includes practices such as swallowing fog, ingesting vapor, culling the light of the sun and moon, drinking the lights of the stars, taking in the energies of the five directions, and culling the energies of water and fire. Some concentrate on imagination of traveling throughout the world. Some imagine the two energies of yin and yang in the body turning into a woman and a man engaging in sexual intercourse. All sorts of artificial visualizations are in the middle middle grade.

3. UPPER MIDDLE GRADE

These methods include formal religious practices such as transmission of initiation and precepts, readings, recitations, and preaching. Also included are such practices as stargazing, bowing to the stars, keeping silent, doing hard labor, and maintaining outward virtues.

These doings are the highest of the middle grade, gradually approaching the Tao. Beyond these are three upper grades.

THREE UPPER GRADES

I. LOWER UPPER GRADE

These methods include such practices as mirror gazing, meditative breathing, massage, physical exercises, extended pronunciation of certain sounds for therapeutic purposes, mentally gazing at the top of the head, keeping the attention on the navel, and swallowing copious amounts of saliva.

Some consider the term "firing process" to mean massaging the body to make it warm. Some seek long life by making nine massage strokes for one forceful exhalation in a rhythmic massage-breathing exercise. Some work up copious saliva and consider that to be what is meant by the technical term "true seed." Some consider a thousand mouthfuls of saliva to be what is meant by the term "enlivening." Some keep the mind on the "elixir fields" in the torso and head, some stare at the nose.

2. MIDDLE UPPER GRADE

These methods include such practices as holding the breath and circulating psychosomatic energy, bending and stretching exercises, massaging the lower back and kidneys, focusing the mind on the forehead, exercising the eyes, twisting the spine, and keeping the mind on the umbilical region.

Some call the eyes "sun and moon." Some consider the point between the eyebrows to be the "mysterious pass." Some chatter the teeth, a concentration exercise, and call that the "gate of heaven." Some imagine the basic spirit going out and in through the top of the head. Some silently pay court to the supreme god. Some consider oblivion to be entry into trance. Some consider counting the breaths to be the "firing process." Some imagine black and white energies of the heart and genitals merging.

3. HIGHER UPPER GRADE

These methods include such practices as exercising vitality and energy, tuning the internal organs, visualizing pure lands, fixedly concentrating on the elixir fields, swallowing the noon sunlight, circulating psychophysical energy through the three elixir fields, rerouting vitality aroused by sexual intercourse or inner concentration so that it travels up the spine to boost the brain, and inward gazing.

There are over a thousand practices in the upper three grades. Mediocre practitioners perform them, and they can thereby ward off sickness. Beyond these are three vehicles of gradual method.

IX.

THREE VEHICLES
OF GRADUAL METHOD

*Refining thought by mind is the firing process. Ceasing thought is
nurturing the fire. Keeping brilliance to oneself is stabilization.
Conquering inner demons is "battle in the field." Body, mind, and
will are the three essentials. The heart of heaven is the
mysterious pass.*

LOWER VEHICLE

In the terminology of this vehicle, body and mind are the alchemical
cauldron and furnace, vitality and energy are the medicinal ingredients,
heart and genitals are fire and water, five internal organs are the five
forces, the liver and lungs are the dragon and tiger, semen is the true seed.

In this system, the "firing process" is carried out in terms of year,
month, day, and hour. Swallowing saliva to irrigate the digestive system
is called "bathing." The mouth and nostrils are considered the "three essentials." The space in front of the kidneys and behind the navel is considered the "mysterious pass." The merging of the five forces is considered completion of the "elixir pill."

This is a method of comfort and bliss that includes over a hundred operations. If one can forget feelings, this can also nurture life. This is somewhat similar to the higher three grades mentioned above, but the application is different.

MIDDLE VEHICLE

According to the usage of this vehicle, HEAVEN ☰ and EARTH ☷ are the cauldron and furnace, WATER ☵ and FIRE ☲ are water and fire, sun and moon are the medicinal ingredients. The five forces are vitality, spirit, higher soul, lower soul, and will. The tiger and dragon are body and mind. Energy is the true seed.

The seasons of cold and heat of a year are the firing process. Showering with holy water is bathing. Inward states not going out, external objects not getting in, is "stabilization." The head, solar plexus, and pubis are the three essentials. The top center of the brain is the mysterious pass. The merging of vitality and spirit is the completion of the elixir pill.

This middle vehicle is a method for nurturing life; it includes dozens of operations. It is much like the lower vehicle. Practiced diligently, it can prolong life.

HIGHER VEHICLE

According to the usage of this vehicle, heaven and earth are the cauldron and furnace, sun and moon are fire and water, yin and yang are the mechanism of evolution. "Lead," "mercury," "silver," "sand," and "earth" are the five elements. Essence and sense are the dragon and tiger. Thought is the true seed.

Refining thought by mind is the firing process. Ceasing thought is nurturing the fire. Keeping brilliance to oneself is "stabilization." Conquering inner demons is "battle in the field." Body, mind, and will are the three essentials. The heart of heaven is the mysterious pass. Sense coming back to essence is completion of the elixir pill. Being suffused with harmonious energy is bathing.

This is the higher-vehicle path of extending life. There are resemblances to the middle vehicle in it, but the application is not the same. There are a dozen or so items involved. When superior practitioners carry this out consistently from beginning to end, they can realize the Way of immortals.

X.

THE HIGHEST VEHICLE

When accomplishment is fulfilled, character is well developed, and one directly transcends to completion all at once; physically and spiritually sublimated, one merges with the Tao in reality.

The highest vehicle is the ineffable Way of supreme ultimate reality. Here cosmic space is the cauldron, the absolute is the furnace. Clear serenity is the foundation of the elixir pill, nondoing is the matrix of the elixir pill.

Essence and life are the lead and mercury. Concentration and insight are water and fire, controlling desire and anger is the mixing of water and fire. Unification of essence and sense is the combining of metal and wood. Cleaning the mind is bathing. Maintaining sincerity and settling the will is stabilization.

Discipline, concentration, and insight are the three essentials. The center is the mysterious pass. Clarifying the mind is miraculous experience. Seeing the essence of mind is crystallization. Merging of the three bases into one is the spiritual embryo. Unification of essence and life is the completion of the elixir pill. Having a body outside the body is release from the matrix. Breaking through space is perfect attainment.

The subtlety of this supreme vehicle can be practiced by the most developed people. When accomplishment is fulfilled, character is well developed and one directly transcends to completion all at once; physically and spiritually sublimated, one merges with the Tao in reality.

XI.

DIALOGUES:
The Underlying Unity of Taoism, Confucianism, and Buddhism

Forgetting feelings to nurture essence, emptying the mind to nurture the spirit, myriad entanglements cease at once, a hundred thoughts clear up. Body and mind unstirring, the spirit congeals and energy crystallizes—this is called the alchemical foundation, and is also metaphorically referred to as the spiritual embryo.

One night the Master of the Brilliant Moon was sitting peacefully in the moon cave. The cold light and clear air were pure and pleasant. His disciple, Master of the Jadelike Moon, was reflecting intensely on the importance of the matter of life and death, the necessity of respectfully seeking out spiritual immortals, and the need for concentrated cultivation. He asked the teacher, "I have heard that the elevated sages, the lofty realized ones, the immortal teachers since ancient times, have all attained the Tao by cultivation of reality and have always considered lead and mercury the root and stem of the gold pill. What are lead and mercury?"

The teacher said, "Lead and mercury are the beginning of heaven and earth, the mother of myriad beings, the basis of the gold pill. They are not the metals ordinarily referred to by these names.

"Nevertheless, people in error, ignorant of the true mystery, thinking in terms of their own arbitrary ideas, have confused and ruined later students, so that they have wasted their lives. This is a great pity. Without the guidance of a genuine teacher, whatever you do is arbitrary. This is what the adept Ziyang meant when he wrote, 'Even if you are exceptionally intelligent, if you do not meet a real teacher, don't indulge in guesswork.'

"Now I will point out to you the true lead and true mercury—they are body and mind. A wise teacher said, 'Body and mind are the medicine and fire.' Also, 'If you want to know the river source where the medicine is produced, it's just in the southwest—this is its homeland.' Southwest is the direction associated with the *I Ching* trigram EARTH ☷. EARTH is associated with the body. The vitality in the body is yang within yin. This is likened to the center line of HEAVEN ☰ entering EARTH ☷ to make WATER ☵. Yin outside, yang inside—there is the metal of HEAVEN in WATER, so it is called metal in water. This stands for sense in vitality.

"Now mercury is the energy in the mind, yin within yang. It is likened to the center line of EARTH ☷ entering HEAVEN ☰ to make FIRE ☲. Yang outside, yin inside, firm outside, flexible inside, HEAVEN outside, EARTH inside—there is EARTH within FIRE, so it is called mercury in cinnabar. This stands for essence in consciousness.

"It is because of the subtlety of the psychic combination of vitality and energy that the images of lead and mercury are used symbolically. It is just to make the student aware that there are substance and function. Thinking along these lines, it is all a matter of body and mind. After body and mind are united, there is no more 'lead and mercury.' "

QUESTION: What is "extracting and adding"?

ANSWER: When the body does not stir, the energy is settled; this is called

41

"extraction." When the mind does not stir, the spirit is settled; this is called "addition." When body and mind do not stir, the spirit congeals and the energy crystallizes; this is called "returning to the basis."

Therefore "extracting lead and adding mercury" means taking the yang in the center of WATER ☵ to fill in the yin in the center of FIRE ☲, thus forming HEAVEN ☰. That means taking the true sense submerged in the earthly out of the earthly in order to eliminate the mundanity which has invaded the essence of mind through conditioning, thus resulting in restoration of the primal celestial state of conscious energy.

QUESTION: What is "cooking and refining"?

ANSWER: When body and mind are on the verge of unification, if there is the slightest disturbance, then you use a firm, resolute mind to oppose it; this is called "martial refining." Once body and mind are unified, after vitality and energy have commingled, you use a flexible, peaceful mind to preserve this; this is called "cultural cooking."

The principle of this is nothing but conquering body and mind—this is what is called "cooking lead and refining mercury." Forgetting feelings to nurture essence, emptying the mind to nurture the spirit, myriad entanglements cease at once, a hundred thoughts clear up. Body and mind unstirring, the spirit congeals and energy crystallizes—this is called the alchemical foundation and is also metaphorically referred to as the spiritual embryo.

The different terms mentioned above simply refer to using essence to concentrate sense. When your nature is tranquil, feelings are forgotten; you see the original, embrace the fundamental, revert to openness, go back to the root, return to Life. This is called completion of the elixir pill and is metaphorically called release from the matrix.

QUESTION: The alchemical classics say that the essence of the work is in the mysterious pass. Where is the mysterious pass?

ANSWER: The mysterious pass is the most recondite and subtle mechanism. How could it have a fixed position? If you place it in the body, that is wrong; yet it is also wrong to seek it outside the body. To cling to the body is to be fixated on the physical form; to cling to externals is to be fixated on things.

The mysterious pass is just the point where the physical elements and five forces do not adhere. Let me give you a simile to facilitate understanding. The movements of a marionette are a matter of the mechanism at the top of the strings, which is operated by the puppeteer. The marionette is like the physical body, the strings are like the mysterious pass, and the puppeteer working the strings is like the original true nature.

Without the strings, the marionette cannot move; without the mysterious pass, people cannot move. You should concentrate twenty-four hours a day, throughout all your activities, on inwardly searching for this: what is it that speaks, is silent, looks and listens?

If body and mind are tranquil and settled, and the heart is still, you will naturally see the mysterious pass where the true potential subtly responds. When the *I Ching* says "tranquil and unstirring," it is referring to the essence of the mysterious pass; when it says "sensitive and effective," it is referring to the function of the mysterious pass.

Having seen the mysterious pass, once you attain it you have attained it forever. The medicines, the firing process, the three bases, and the eight trigrams are all therein.

If people today consider some physical location to be the mysterious pass, they will not attain, no matter how hard they work. I would like to point it out directly, but I'm afraid you wouldn't believe and wouldn't be able to use it. You must see it for yourself.

It is like the learning of the primordial in Confucianism—it is necessary to recognize it tacitly. Mencius said, "The vast energy fills the universe—it is hard to tell of." Isn't the subtlety that is hard to tell of the mysterious pass?

In Buddhism, the special transmission outside doctrine, which does not establish literal formulation, requires people to take it in with the spirit and understand it in the mind—this is called the incommunicable subtlety. If you know this principle, you can merge all through one penetration.

QUESTION: Some say that by practice of Buddhism and Taoism one can end birth and death and get out of routine existence, but by studying Confucianism one can fulfill social ethics yet not understand birth and death. Is this not the difference between Buddhism and Taoism on the one hand and Confucianism on the other?

ANSWER: How can those who arrive at truth worry about birth and death? There is a Confucian saying, "Find out truth and fulfill human nature, thereby arriving at the destiny of life; getting to the root of beginnings, returning to ends, knowledge encompasses myriad things." This is talking about knowing birth and death. What in Taoism is called the study of essence and life is actually the true message of Confucianism, where it is called the study of human nature and destiny.

Furthermore, when the ancient sage chieftain Fu Xi first wrote the *I Ching* signs, setting up teaching embodying the celestial, using the Tao to develop people, there was no division into three teachings. Therefore it is said, "The Supreme Celestial has not two ways, sages have not two minds."

The first line drawn by Fu Xi represents the absolute. When there is one, then there are two; this represents the two modes, one yang, one yin. "One yin and one yang—this is called the Tao." Looking up, gazing at the sky, Fu Xi wrote a line to represent heaven; looking down, examining the earth, he wrote a line to represent earth. In between he wrote a line to represent humankind.

Therefore three solid lines form the trigram HEAVEN, representing the "three components"—heaven, earth, and humanity. Two HEAVENs separated, making three broken lines, form EARTH, representing the six parts—the members of the body and the directions of space.

So it is said that the Tao establishing heaven is yin and yang, the Tao establishing earth is flexibility and firmness, and the Tao establishing humankind is benevolence and justice. The three components each have two aspects, so six lines form EARTH.

Speaking in terms of the person, the Tao establishing heaven being yin and yang refers to the spirit and energy of the mind; the Tao establishing earth being flexibility and firmness refers to the form and substance of the body; the Tao establishing humankind being benevolence and justice refers to the essence and sense of the will.

Mind, body, and will are represented by the three components of HEAVEN; spirit, energy, essence, sense, form, and substance are represented by the six parts of EARTH. This is what the *I Ching* means when it says, "Find it afar in things, find it nearby in the body."

QUESTION: The Connected Sayings commentary in the *I Ching* says six lines make a hexagram; why do you say six lines make the trigram EARTH?
ANSWER: When it says six lines make a hexagram, it refers to the hexagrams which the ancient King Wen made by doubling the trigrams invented by Fu Xi in high antiquity. But it cannot be said that there were no three components and six parts before King Wen doubled the trigrams into hexagrams.

A sage of yore said that "the Tao establishing heaven is yin and yang" refers to the HEAVEN and EARTH of the celestial plane, "the Tao establishing earth is flexibility and firmness" refers to the HEAVEN and EARTH of the terrestrial plane, and "the Tao establishing humankind is humanity and justice" refers to the HEAVEN and EARTH of the human dimension.

If you think along these lines, the three components and six parts are contained in the two trigrams HEAVEN and EARTH. The statement that six lines make a hexagram means after the doubling of the trigrams; this is called the temporal dimension.

QUESTION: You may say the three components and six parts were there before the hexagrams, but the *I Ching* commentary says that the *I Ching* images are important for fashioning instruments: were the images established based on instruments, or were instruments fashioned based on the images?
ANSWER: Instruments were fashioned based on the images.

45

QUESTION: After the august chieftains of high antiquity, later sages of ancient times fashioned instruments, but in each case the *I Ching* commentary refers to it in terms of the hexagrams. You say instruments were fashioned based on the images of the hexagrams, but were the names of the hexagrams in existence before King Wen doubled the trigrams?

ANSWER: You're on the wrong track. A past sage said, "You should believe that there were the Changes to begin with, before the diagrams." So the sixty-four hexagrams represented in the *I Ching* were all there in reality itself before King Wen doubled the trigrams.

QUESTION: If there are sixty-four hexagrams without doubling the trigrams, then why did King Wen double them?

ANSWER: The permutation into sixty-four hexagrams without doubling trigrams is the mental teaching of Fu Xi, the true transmission of the unifying thread of the Tao, leading students of all times to the door of enlightenment.

The production of the sixty-four hexagrams by doubling the trigrams is the consummation of the social studies of King Wen, his son the Duke of Zhou, and the great educator Confucius. Their purpose was to correct human standards, so that people of the world would take to the good and avoid the bad, establishing a stable structure of social relations.

Though one dare not carelessly express the science of essence and life, or human nature and destiny, nevertheless it is unacceptable to conceal this Tao. Confucius revealed it slightly in his *I Ching* commentaries, and the Taoist-Confucian noumenalist Zhou Dunyi clarified it in his writing on the absolute. They wanted people to think carefully and thoroughly and understand it for themselves. This is the kind of study that keeps the knowledge alive.

QUESTION: How do you explain the statement, "One yin and one yang constitute the Tao"?

ANSWER: Yin and yang are HEAVEN and EARTH. HEAVEN and EARTH come from the absolute; the absolute bifurcates into the two modes; the two modes are the celestial and the terrestrial.

46

QUESTION: HEAVEN ☰ is yang, EARTH ☷ is yin; why do you also speak of the celestial and terrestrial using the ordinary terms for heaven and earth?

ANSWER: The celestial and the terrestrial are HEAVEN and EARTH; HEAVEN and EARTH are yin and yang; yin and yang are one absolute; the absolute is basically infinite.

When we speak in terms of the absolute, we say "celestial" and "terrestrial." When we speak in terms of the Changes as represented by the *I Ching*, we say HEAVEN and EARTH. When we speak in terms of the Tao we say yin and yang.

In terms of the human being, the celestial and the terrestrial are form and substance, HEAVEN and EARTH are sense and essence, yin and yang are spirit and energy.

In terms of technical symbolism, the celestial is called the dragon, the terrestrial is called the tiger; HEAVEN is called the horse, EARTH is called the cow; yang is called the raven, yin is called the rabbit.

In terms of alchemy, the celestial is the cauldron, the terrestrial is the furnace; HEAVEN is metal, EARTH is earth; yin is mercury, yang is lead.

Spoken of separately, there are various different names, but in sum they are one yin and one yang. When people who cultivate immortality forge lead and mercury into a pill of the elixir immortality, this means that the body and mind combine and return to the beginning, yin and yang combine and revert to the absolute.

QUESTION: A commentary in the *I Ching* says, "Heaven and earth establish their positions, and the Changes go on therein." What does this mean?

ANSWER: Heaven and earth establish their positions, humankind is born therein; these are called the three components. Therefore people and things are born again and again, without cease. The reason it does not say people and things, but instead says the Changes, is that the sages say HEAVEN and EARTH are the door of the Changes, and the Tao is followed by adapting to the time.

In alchemy, HEAVEN and EARTH are called the cauldron and furnace—this is "heaven and earth establishing their positions." Yin and yang are called the evolutionary mechanism—this is "the Changes going on therein." Gathering medicine from the origin endlessly is carrying out the firing process unceasingly.

QUESTION: It is also written, "Opening the door is called HEAVEN, closing the door is called EARTH; one opening and one closing is called Change." What does this mean?

ANSWER: "One opening and one closing" is one movement and one stillness. The yang of HEAVEN and the yin of EARTH are like the opening and closing of a door; this is the passageway of Changes of HEAVEN and EARTH.

Yin and yang alternate movement and stillness, work and rest go on and on; origin, development, fruition, and consummation establish the four seasons and make a year. Change means transformation.

The ultimate Tao and spirit and energy, as an undifferentiated unity, pervade the universe and all beings, opening and closing endlessly, producing the macrocosm and the microcosm.

Speaking in terms of the human body, this is breathing. Breathing out, one contacts the root of heaven—this is called opening. Breathing in, one contacts the root of earth—this is called closing. One exhalation and one inhalation produce the "gold liquid," the combination of energy and spirit—this is called change.

Opening and closing, breathing out and breathing in, are the "door of the mysterious female," the root of heaven and earth. Here "breathing out" and "breathing in" do not refer to exhalation and inhalation through the nose, but rather to the opening and closing of the true breath, the inner pulse of life, the movement of energy and stillness of spirit.

QUESTION: It is written, "The metaphysical is called the Tao, the physical is called the vessel." What does this mean?

ANSWER: The metaphysical has no form or substance. The physical has body and function. That which has no form or substance is connected to essence; this is called "mercury." That which has body and function is connected to life; this is called "lead." In sum, these are no more than body and mind.

QUESTION: It is written, "The sages used the Changes to clean their hearts, and withdrew into recondite secrecy." What does this mean?
ANSWER: It is the consummation of sincerity and truthfulness. The principles of the Changes extend throughout the macrocosm and the microcosm; sages ponder the principles of the Changes to clean their hearts and thoughts, and store them in ultimate sincerity.

QUESTION: The Classic of Documents says, "The human mind is perilous, the mind of Tao is subtle. Precise and unified, hold to the center." How does one hold to the center?
ANSWER: "Holding" refers to consistent stability. The "center" is the balance of straightforwardness. The mind of Tao is subtle and hard to see, the human mind is perilous and unstable. Even perfected people have the human mind, and even ignoramuses have the mind of Tao. If one can keep the mind constantly balanced in straightforwardness, this is what makes it subtle and hard to see. If the mind is even slightly biased and unbalanced, this is what makes it perilous and unstable.

Students of immortality discern unity and keep to it without vacillation, always holding to the center. Then naturally the perilous becomes safe and the subtle becomes obvious. This is also the reason why in spiritual alchemy the center is taken to be the mysterious pass.

QUESTION: It is written, "The work of heaven above is imperceptible." What does this mean?
ANSWER: The manifestation of truth may be imperceptible, but the Way of Heaven cannot be hidden either. When Taoist scripture speaks of the profound mystery of the macrocosm, this too is in reference to the supreme reality.

QUESTION: What is "unconsciously following the laws of God"?

ANSWER: Sages know it by nature and follow it silently. The celestial design is what is called the natural Tao in which noncontrivance is attained, which is realized without thought and reached without striving. This is what the classic on Equilibrium in the Center calls truthfulness and illumination.

When those who study the Tao already have the capacity, they directly comprehend essence and naturally comprehend life. This is knowing by nature. Those of shallower capacity are unable to comprehend essence directly; they penetrate it by way of teaching, going from being into nonbeing, from the coarse to the subtle. Therefore they first comprehend life and then comprehend essence afterward. This is knowing by learning.

QUESTION: It is said that Confucius was happy even in poverty—wherein lay his happiness?

ANSWER: Confucius was pleased with heaven and knew destiny. Therefore he did not worry. Even when oppressed he still enjoyed himself with music and song. He had attained a state not far from realization of the Changes. He also cultivated himself to restore vision of the heart of heaven and earth, and investigated truth to fulfill human nature and arrive at the meaning of life. This is the marvel of spiritual alchemy.

QUESTION: What about Confucius' great pupil Yan Hui's happiness in poverty?

ANSWER: Yan Hui had learned Confucius' way of satisfaction with the celestial design, knowledge of destiny, and freedom from anxiety. Therefore nothing affected his happiness. So he was like a simpleton, practicing psychological fasting, sitting and forgetting, getting rid of idle intellectualism, nearly becoming empty repeatedly. This too is the marvel of spiritual alchemy.

QUESTION: Zi Lu, another disciple, asked Confucius about death, and Confucius replied, "As long as you don't know life, how can you know death?" What does this mean?

ANSWER: Life and death are like the regularity of day and night; when you know there is day, you know there is night. The *I Ching* speaks of finding out the beginning and returning to the end; thus do we know about death and life.

Alchemical literature says that the state before birth is the basis of the gold pill. Buddhism has us ask where our essence was before our bodies existed.

Looking at it in this way, we see that the point of entry of Confucianism, Taoism, and Buddhism just requires us to find out the beginning, whereupon we will spontaneously know the end, to go back to the source and know the source.

If people can find out where this being comes from, they will naturally know the whole of life and death.

Consider the absolute: prior to the bifurcation of the absolute into yin and yang, what is this? If you can penetrate this, then you will know the state before embodiment. Finding out the beginning, you can thereby comprehend the end.

QUESTION: Before the absolute bifurcates, its form is like an egg. What is outside the egg?
ANSWER: The great void. When people receive energy, and their form and substance are still undifferentiated, they are also like eggs. After they are born, human nature and destiny are established. Outside the body is all the great void.

QUESTION: Confucius said, "My way is permeated by unity." What does this mean?
ANSWER: Sages say the unique celestial design in one's being permeates the universe, including all philosophies and religions and all things. This is like the Buddhist principle of nonabsoluteness of self, person, being, and soul. It is also like the Taoist teaching of comprehending everything by comprehending one. In all of these there is a pervasive unity.

QUESTION: According to the legend of the founding of Chan Buddhism, once Buddha held up a flower before an assembly, and his disciple Mahakasyapa alone smiled. Buddha said, "I have the treasury of vision of truth, the ineffable mind of nirvana—this I entrust to Mahakasyapa." What was this smile?

ANSWER: When Buddha held up the flower before the assembly, no one but Mahakasyapa saw the enlightened mind. Only Mahakasyapa perceived the subtlety of the enlightened mind; that is why he smiled. Therefore Buddha entrusted to Mahakasyapa the marvel that is beyond doctrine.

QUESTION: Bodhidharma, the founder of Chan Buddhism in China, came to China from India and directly pointed to mind, without setting up verbal formulations, so people would see essence and attain enlightenment. What is seeing essence?

ANSWER: Bodhidharma pointed directly to mind with the subtle principle of true emptiness. Seeing essence makes people turn things around so that feelings are empty and they spontaneously see the essence of mind. It cannot be communicated in words.

QUESTION: Confucians have the primordial *I Ching*, Buddhists have the Perfection of Wisdom scriptures, and Taoists have the Spiritual Jewel scriptures—are these not words?

ANSWER: No. They are all cases of sages using the wordless to make formulations in words revealing the true eternal Tao. The Buddhist canon and records of sayings of adepts, the Confucian classics, traditions, and philosophical treatises, and the Taoist scriptures and alchemical texts are all pathways for entry into the Tao, ladders for climbing into the transcendental. If you reach the ultimate point, then not even a single word can be applied.

Your questioning about these various matters is also like a raft to cross a river—the transcendent experience should be sought outside of verbal formulations. If you encounter it, understand it, and penetrate it, you return to the absolute, with complete illumined awareness shining, unobstructed penetrating consciousness. Once essence and life are both complete, form and spirit both sublimated, being one with space, on a par with immortals and Buddhas, will not be hard.

QUESTION: I gratefully accept your revelation of the unifying principle of the three teachings of Buddhism, Taoism, and Confucianism, but it seems to me that there is a difference between Buddhist nirvana and Taoist "release from the matrix."

ANSWER: Nirvana and release from the matrix are but one principle. Release from the matrix means shedding the matrix of mundanity—isn't this nirvana? Taoists refine vitality into energy, refine energy into spirit, refine spirit into emptiness, then embrace the fundamental and return to openness—this is the same principle as the Buddhist teaching of ultimate emptiness, no different.

QUESTION: Is there still evolution after release from the matrix?

ANSWER: There is evolution. A sage has said, "Having a body outside the body is still no marvel; only when space is shattered is complete reality revealed." So after release from the matrix, one should tread the ground of reality until one unites with space.

When Buddhists speak of true emptiness, Confucians of noncontrivance, and Taoists of spontaneity, all are referring to embracing the fundamental, returning to the origin, and uniting with cosmic space. People with fixations cannot know this Way that is permeated with unity.

XII.

QUESTIONS AND ANSWERS

Use action and stillness for the cauldron and furnace, vitality and energy for water and fire, body and mind for the evolutionary mechanism, essence and sense for the medicinal ingredients.

The teacher said to Zhao Ding-an, "The teachers of former generations, the elevated realized ones, the exalted sages, had a way to supreme reality, and left traditions on it in the world to liberate people—do you know?"

Ding-an said, "I have just entered the mystic school and am completely ignorant. I am very fortunate to have been taken on as a disciple. I really do not know the Tao of supreme true reality, and hope you will teach me."

The teacher said, "The Tao of supreme true reality has no limit that can be surpassed. It is the mystery of mysteries; no image can describe it. It is so without affirmation. It refers to the ultimate, supreme wonder. Sages have called it the Tao.

"All of the superior immortals since antiquity have realized mastery by way of this Tao; their practice and experience have always been based on this. The teaching of spiritual alchemy, which has been handed on privately, through verbal instruction and mind-to-mind communication by enlightened teachers over the generations, is this sublime Tao of supreme true reality."

QUESTION: What is the reason for using the image of a "gold pill" to symbolize the marvel of supreme true reality?

ANSWER: "Gold" means stability, the "pill" means roundness. Buddhists represent this as complete awareness, Confucians represent it as the absolute. It is nothing but the original unified consciousness. Its fundamental true essence, like the stability of gold, like the roundness of a pill, never ever decays. The more it is refined, the brighter it becomes. This is symbolized by a circle, which Buddhists call true suchness, Confucians call the absolute, and we Taoists call the gold pill. The names are different, but the essence is the same.

The *I Ching* says Change has an absolute, which gives birth to two modes. The absolute refers to open nonreified nature; the two modes are yin and yang. Yin and yang are heaven and earth, and humanity lives between heaven and earth. These are called the three components.

The Tao of the three components is inherent in one body: the absolute is the basic spirit, the two modes are body and mind. In terms of alchemy, the absolute is the matrix of the pill, the two modes are true lead and true mercury, the sense of real knowledge and the essence of conscious knowledge.

What we call lead and mercury do not refer to substances such as quicksilver, cinnabar, sulfur, tin, or vegetable matter. Nor are they semen, saliva, or the energy and blood of the genitals and heart. They are the basic spirit in the body and the basic energy in the body.

When the body is not agitated, the vital energy congeals; this is represented as an elixir pill. The so-called elixir pill is the body. What is represented by the empty circle is the essence, the true essence: taking the essence from the elixir is called the completion of the pill. The elixir pill is not made with anything external; it is made of the basis of life. This is truly real.

Few people know this. Many do not get the right information and seek externals, pursuing the false and turning their backs on the true. Therefore there are many who study but few who attain.

Some work with minerals, some work with external vapors such as clouds and fog, some work with sunlight and moonlight, some gather starlight, some "make elixir" by visualizing nine pills in the sky, some visualize something in the abdomen and call that the elixir pill, some keep their minds on the point between the eyebrows, some drive the vitality up the spine to boost the brain, some convey energy into the umbilical region.

And there are many other practices—ingesting filth, drinking semen and menstrual blood, breathing exercises, physical exercises, psychosomatic exercises, refining hormones from urine, bending and stretching and massage, silently paying court to the supreme god, circulating energy through the torso and head—there are more than a thousand such minor techniques, which will not accomplish the great result even if practiced diligently. This is what is meant by the classic statement, "Correct method is hard to find—many miss the true way and many enter abberant schools."

The essentials of arriving at reality are utterly simple, utterly easy; difficult to find, but easy to accomplish. None would fail to achieve it if they were guided by perfected people.

QUESTION: Please instruct me.

ANSWER: Refining the gold pill is all a matter of taking over the creative evolution of heaven and earth. Use action and stillness for the cauldron and furnace, vitality and energy for water and fire, body and mind for the evolutionary mechanism, essence and sense for the medicinal ingredients. Keep centered on mindfulness of the celestial, find the mysterious pass, gather the vital energy of the sense of essence at the appropriate time, then withdraw into watchful passivity in the proper manner.

Unify essence, sense, spirit, vitality, and will. Keep a balanced proportion of firmness and flexibility, creativity and receptivity, movement and stillness. With a combination of will and the inner sense of true essence, return to the fundamental, go back to the basis, revert to the root, and return to Life. When the work is complete and the spirit is prepared, the ordinary is shed and one becomes an immortal. This is called the completion of the elixir pill.

The most hidden and subtle mechanism is the mysterious pass. Why don't the alchemical classics say just where the mysterious pass is? It is for the very reason that it is indescribable and inexplicable that it is called the mysterious pass. Therefore sages have just used the word "center" to point it out to people. The mysterious pass is indicated by the word "center."

This "center" does not mean center in the sense of inside as opposed to outside, nor does it mean center in terms of location in the center of the four directions. Buddhists say, "When you don't think good or bad, what are you basically like?" This is the center of Chan. Confucians say, "When emotions are not active, this is called the center." This is the center of Confucianism. Taoists say, "Where thoughts do not arise is called the center." This is the center of Taoism. This is the center as applied by the three teachings.

When the *I Ching* says "tranquil, unperturbed," this is the substance of the center; "sensitive and effective" is the function of the center.

Lao-tzu says, "Effecting utter emptiness, keeping complete silence, as myriad things act in concert, I thereby watch the return."

The *I Ching* says, "Return means seeing the heart of heaven and earth."

The *I Ching* hexagram RETURN ☷☳ consists of one yang __ arising under five yins _ _: yin is quietude, yang is movement; when quietude reaches its consummation, it gives rise to movement. It is this point of movement that is the mysterious pass.

Just apply your attention to the point where you rouse the mind and activate thought, concentrating on this constantly—then the mysterious pass will spontaneously appear. When you see the mysterious pass, then the medicinal ingredients, the firing process, the operation, extracting and adding, all the way to release from the matrix and spiritual transformation, are all in this one opening.

Gathering medicine means gathering the true sense of the essence of consciousness within oneself. This is done by first quieting the mind to still the impulses of arbitrary feelings; when stillness is perfected, there is a movement of unconditioned energy. This is the energy of true sense, and its first movement arising from stillness is called the return of yang. This is to be fostered until sense and essence, energy and spirit, are united. After that, withdraw into watchful passivity, because if you persist in intensive concentration after the point of sufficiency, your work will be wasted.

Thus the cycle of work goes from movement to stillness to movement to stillness. With long perseverance in practice, there takes place a gradual solidification, a gradual crystallization, which is the stabilization of real consciousness. This is described as nonsubstance producing substance, and it is represented as a spiritual embryo. This is called completion of the elixir.

QUESTION: You have told me about the process of the work, but I don't know all the different terms—please instruct me.

ANSWER: The different terms are just symbols—none are beyond body and mind. When you are working, stilling the senses and tuning the breath, physically immobile, and you cause the vitality, spirit, higher soul, lower soul, and will each to rest in its own proper place, this is called the "five energies returning to the basis."

When the mind does not move, this is called "the dragon howling." When the body does not move, this is called "the tiger roaring." Not moving physically or mentally is called "overcoming the dragon and subduing the tiger." When the dragon howls, the energy is stable; when the tiger roars, the vitality is stable.

Vitality and energy are symbolized by a snake and a tortoise, body and mind by a tiger and a dragon. Uniting these is called "combining the four signs."

Concentrating sense through essence is called "metal and wood joining." Controlling energy by vitality is called "water and fire mixing."

Wood and fire have the same source, their natures are one; their associated numbers add up to five. Water and metal have the same source, their natures are one; their associated numbers also add up to five. The chamber of earth, in the center, is assigned the number five. When mind, body, and will unite, these three sets meet and form the "infant." This is called the merging of the three fives.

Refining vitality into energy, refining energy into spirit, refining spirit back into openness—this is called "the three flowers gathered on the peak." It is also called the three passes.

Many students now refer to the coccyx, midspine, and back of the head as the three passes. This is just a method of practice, in which the attention is focused on these three sensitive areas and psychic energy is sent through them along the spinal column. This is not quintessential.

The point of arousing the mind and activating thought is the "mysterious female." People who refer to the mysterious female as the mouth and nose, relating it to ordinary respiration, are incorrect.

Body, mind, and will are the three essentials. The essence in the mind is called "mercury within cinnabar." The energy in the body is called "metal in water."

Not letting external objects in, not letting inner states out—this is called "stable settlement."

Being tranquil and unperturbed is called "nurturing the fire." Open, nonreifying spontaneity is called "operation."

Maintaining sincerity and focusing the will is called "guarding the castle."

Conquering inner demons is called "battle in the field."

True mercury is called the girl, true lead is called the boy. The embryonic breath is called the go-between. Essence and sense are called husband and wife.

Cleaning the mind and stabilizing the will, the essence is tranquil and the spirit is aware; yin and yang combine, the three bases convene—this is called "completing the embryo."

Carefully protecting the spiritual root is called "incubation." Incubation is like a dragon nurturing a pearl, like a hen sitting on her eggs; one carefully guards against straying, for with the slightest slip all the work that has gone before is wasted.

Luminous spirit emerging from the shell is called "release from the matrix." Returning to the root, returning to Life, going back to the original beginning, is called "transcendent liberation." Breaking through space is called "perfect attainment."

QUESTION: When the gold pill is completed, can it be seen?
ANSWER: It can be seen.

QUESTION: Does it have form?
ANSWER: It has no form.

QUESTION: If it has no form, how can it be seen?
ANSWER: "Gold pill" is just a name. How could it have form? I say it can be seen, but it cannot be seen with the eyes. In Buddhism it is said, "In not seeing, one sees intimately; in intimate seeing, one does not see." A Taoist scripture says, "When you look at it, you don't see it; when you listen for it, you don't hear it. This is called the Tao."

Looking at it, you don't see it, yet never are you not seeing it; listening for it, you don't hear it, yet never are you not hearing it. To say it can be seen and heard does not mean it is within the reach of eye and ear—it is only seen by the mind, heard by the will.

For a simile, let us take the example of the wind: in the mountains it makes the trees sway, on the water it rouses waves, so we cannot say it is not there; yet we cannot see it or grasp it, so in that sense we cannot say it is there.

So it is also with the substance of the gold pill. Therefore in the beginning of refinement of the pill elixir, being and nonbeing work together, movement and stillness need each other. Then when you accomplish the work, all entanglements abruptly cease, all things are empty, movement and stillness are both forgotten, being and nonbeing are both gone.

Now the mystic pearl takes shape, and the great unity returns to reality. Essence and life both complete, physically and mentally sublimated, one leaves reification and enters nonreification, roams in the clouds, and realizes incorruptible immortality.

Thus the scriptures and alchemical writings use various different terms to lead students from the crude to the subtle, so that they may gradually enter a state of beatitude and then see essence and realize openness.

The actuality is not on paper; writings are like a boat to ferry people across a river—once the people are on the other shore, the boat has no more use. This is the point of the saying of the ancient sage Zhuangzi, "When you catch the rabbit you forget the trap, when you snare the fish you forget the net."

And now that I have said all this to you, you should not cling to the words; just savor the meaning thoroughly and search out the root source. If your mind opens up at a word, it will not be hard to enter right into the realm of noncontrivance.

But there is still a mechanism beyond, which is not easy to set forth lightly—you should seek it outside words.

XIII.

SOME QUESTIONS
ON ALCHEMY

The three passes are the workings of the three bases. Refining vitality into energy is the first pass, refining energy into spirit is the middle pass, refining spirit back into openness is the upper pass.

Of all the commentaries of people of later times on the alchemical classics and writings of the adepts, none are useful. Some are attached to physical forms, some cling to verbal formulations, some consider clear purity to be the emptiness of suffering, some think mercury and lead have form. Their views are not the same—how could people who came after them not be confused? They still do not know the ultimate Tao is one—how could there be two?

Moreover, what are compiled in alchemical books of recent times are mostly sidetracks; their interpretations of "seven-reversion," "nine-restoration," and numerical sequences, for example, are mistaken. So here I have taken the essence of alchemical literature and assembled a number of questions to break through confusion.

QUESTION: What does "nine-restoration" mean?
ANSWER: Nine is the number associated with metal, which symbolizes sense. Restoration means return to the basis. So "nine-restoration"

means using essence to concentrate sense. This is what alchemical literature means when it says, "When metal first returns to essence, then it can be called restored elixir." "Nine-restoration" does not refer to an enumeration of a series.

QUESTION: What does "seven-reversion" mean?
ANSWER: Seven is the number associated with fire, which symbolizes the spirit. Reversion means reversion to the fundamental. So "seven-reversion" means refining the spirit back into openness. Here again, "seven-reversion" does not mean enumeration of a series. This is what the classic *Understanding Reality* means when it says, "Stop enumeration, just get the five forces in proper order."

QUESTION: What are the "three passes"?
ANSWER: The three passes are the workings of the three bases. Refining vitality into energy is the first pass, refining energy into spirit is the middle pass, refining spirit back into openness is the upper pass.

Some call the coccyx, midspine, and back of the head the "three passes," but this just refers to a method of practice and is not utterly essential. That which is essential to ascend to reality is in the three passes—how could they have fixed locations? It is a matter for personal instruction.

QUESTION: What is the "mysterious pass"?
ANSWER: The mysterious pass is the most abstruse, most subtle mechanism. It has no fixed location. Nowadays many people indicate the umbilical sphere, or the top of the head, or the forehead, or the space between the kidneys and genitals, or the space in front of the kidneys and behind the navel. These are all sidetracks.

An alchemical text says, "The opening of the mysterious pass is not to the right or the left, not in front or back, not above or below, not on the inside or outside, not on either side, not in the middle. It is the point where the physical elements and five forces do not adhere."

QUESTION: What are the "three chambers"?

ANSWER: The three chambers are the abodes of the three bases. Spirit resides in the chamber of HEAVEN, energy resides in the central chamber, and vitality resides in the chamber of EARTH. The chamber of HEAVEN, the abode of spirit, is also called the chamber of the purple climax; the central chamber is also called the yellow room; the chamber of EARTH, the abode of vitality, is also called the mansion on the crimson hill. People nowadays who define the three chambers as the "three elixir fields" in the lower abdomen, solar plexus, and brain are incorrect.

QUESTION: What are the "three essentials"?

ANSWER: The three essentials are the opening of returning to the root, the pass of returning to Life, and the valley of open nonreification.

QUESTION: What is the "mysterious female"?

ANSWER: As the *Tao Te Ching* says, "The valley spirit not dying is called the mysterious female." The adept Ziyang said, "The place where thought arises is called the mysterious female." This is correct. I say the place where thought arises is the root of birth and death—is this not the mysterious female? Even so, this only indicates a method of practice; the supreme vehicle is a matter for personal instruction.

QUESTION: What is the "true seed"?

ANSWER: The true seed is the point of spiritual light which is prior to the dichotomization of heaven and earth. Some say people are born from energy, and therefore consider energy the true seed. Some say this body exists due to thought, so they consider thought to be the true seed. Some say this body exists due to reception of the female and male vitalities, so they consider vitality to be the true seed. These three explanations seem right, but actually are wrong. This is what Buddhists mean by the saying, "What the ignorant call the original reality is in fact the root of infinite eons of birth and death."

QUESTION: What are the "crucible" and "furnace"?
ANSWER: Mind and body are the crucible and furnace. An alchemical text says, "First take HEAVEN and EARTH for the crucible and furnace, then take the medicines of the raven and rabbit and cook them." HEAVEN is the mind, EARTH is the body. People nowadays who set up an external furnace and crucible are mistaken.

QUESTION: What are the "medicinal ingredients"?
ANSWER: The medicinal ingredients are true lead and true mercury. These are just the original two things, yin and yang. They may be taken to refer to body and mind, sense and essence, or real knowledge and conscious knowledge.

QUESTION: What is "inner medicine," what is "outer medicine"?
ANSWER: The inner and outer medicines are refining vitality, energy, and spirit. The substance is one, but there are two functions. Sexual vitality, metabolic energy, and thinking spirit are all outer medicine. The primordial essential vitality, the energy of open nonreified spaciousness, and the undecaying basic spirit are inner medicine. This is what is meant by the dual function, inner and outer, mentioned in alchemical literature.

QUESTION: The classic *Understanding Reality* says, "Knock on bamboo to call the tortoise to ingest jade mushroom." What does this mean?
ANSWER: Knocking on bamboo means stilling energy; calling the tortoise means concentrating vitality. Refining vitality into energy, using energy to concentrate vitality, vitality and energy merge and crystallize into a "jade mushroom." Ingesting this preserves life.

QUESTION: *Understanding Reality* says, "Strum the lute to call the phoenix to drink from the medicinal spoon." What does this mean?
ANSWER: Strumming the lute means emptying the mind; calling the phoenix means nurturing the spirit. When you empty the mind and nur-

65

ture the spirit, the mind is clear, the spirit is transformed. The medicinal spoon is formed by conjunction of the celestial will and the earthly will; drinking from this makes essence complete and clear.

QUESTION: What is "the five energies returning to the source"?
ANSWER: When the body is not agitated, the vitality is stable—this is represented as water returning to the source. When the mind is not agitated, the energy is stable—this is represented as fire returning to the source. When the essence of consciousness is still, the higher soul remains within—this is represented as metal returning to the source. When the physical constitution is in harmony, the will is settled—this is represented as earth returning to the source. This total state is called the five energies returning to the source.

QUESTION: What is the "yellow woman"?
ANSWER: Yellow is the color associated with the center; woman refers to mother. Myriad beings are born from earth, so earth is the mother of myriad beings, and thus is called the yellow woman. In humans, this is called the embryonic breath, which means the combination of spirit and energy. It also refers to the true will, which stands in the center of mind and body, heaven and earth, and joins them in harmonious union.

QUESTION: What is the "metal man"?
ANSWER: The metal man is another term for true lead, or the firm sense of real knowledge.

QUESTION: What is "real gold"?
ANSWER: Gold is the basic spirit. It never decays, and becomes brighter the more it is refined, so it is called real gold.

QUESTION: What are "child and mother"?
ANSWER: The spirit is the mother of the body. The spirit being hidden in the body is represented as the mother being concealed within the child.

QUESTION: What are "guest and host"?
ANSWER: Essence is the host of the body, the body is the guest. Now we use this body to nurture this essence, so we let body be the host. This is what the classic *Understanding Reality* means when it says, "Let the other be the host, oneself be the guest."

QUESTION: What is "the primordial one energy"?
ANSWER: Before heaven and earth dichotomize, there is just one awareness; this is the point of true yang in the body. Because it is prior to the separation of the celestial and the earthly, it is called primordial.

QUESTION: What are "water and fire"?
ANSWER: In the sky, the moon and the sun are water and fire; in the *I Ching*, peril and awareness are water and fire; in Chan Buddhism, concentration and insight are water and fire. Confucian sages consider luster and luminosity water and fire; medical science refers to the genitals and heart as water and fire; alchemy takes vitality and energy as water and fire.

I now clearly point out that whatever in one's body flames upward is considered fire, and whatever descends and moistens is considered water. All the various names are metaphors used to foster direct experience in learners.

QUESTION: How is it that there is water in fire?
ANSWER: Water stands for the spirit, fire for awareness; water in fire is the spirit in awareness.

QUESTION: How is it that there is fire in water?
ANSWER: Fire in water, in terms of the body, is the energy within vitality.

QUESTION: What is being "settled"?
ANSWER: When water rises and fire descends, that is called being settled.

The *I Ching* says, "There is a lake below a mountain, diminishing: thus does the superior person stop anger and craving." This is the method of settlement: stop anger and fire descends, stop craving and water rises.

QUESTION: What is being "unsettled"?
ANSWER: When you can't stop anger, fire flames upward; when you can't stop craving, water wets below: the fire of ignorance blazes, the waves of the ocean of suffering roll; the water of desire and the fire of intelligence do not mix. This is called being unsettled.

QUESTION: What is "metal and wood joining"?
ANSWER: Sense coming back to essence is called joining. Sense is associated with metal, essence with wood.

QUESTION: What is "separation"?
ANSWER: When feelings pursue things and consciousness follows thoughts, sense and essence diverge—this is called separation.

QUESTION: What are "clarity" and "turbulence"?
ANSWER: Clarity is when the mind does not stir; turbulence is when the mind stirs.

QUESTION: What are the "two eights"?
ANSWER: The contents of one pound—eight ounces of lead, eight ounces of mercury. It is not really a matter of pounds and ounces—the point is that the two things must be equal. An alchemical text says, "After the prior crescent, before the latter crescent, the medicinal ingredients are equal, the power of the fire is complete." This means balanced proportion of yin and yang—the earthly and the celestial, flexibility and firmness, conscious knowledge and real knowledge. This is also represented by the equality of day and night at the equinoxes.

QUESTION: What is "bathing"?
ANSWER: Washing the mind, cleaning out thoughts—this is called bathing.

QUESTION: What is "completion of the elixir pill"?
ANSWER: When body and mind unite, spirit and energy merge, and sense and essence conjoin—this is called completion of the elixir pill. It is represented as a spiritual embryo.

QUESTION: What is "nurturing the fire"?
ANSWER: Stopping thoughts is nurturing the fire.

QUESTION: What is "release from the matrix"?
ANSWER: Having a body outside the body is release from the matrix.

QUESTION: What is "perfect attainment"?
ANSWER: Merging with cosmic space is called perfect attainment. Evolution beyond things is not easy to speak of—it is a matter of people attaining it themselves.

XIV.

LIVE TEACHINGS
ON COMPLETE REALITY

Learning the science of spiritual immortality does not require a lot of doing; the elixir is just a matter of refining the three treasures of vitality, energy, and spirit.

People on the path of Complete Reality should practice the path of Complete Reality. Complete Reality means keeping the basic reality complete. Only when you keep vitality, energy, and spirit complete can it be called complete reality: as soon as there is any lack, it is not complete; as soon as there is any defilement, it is not real.

By keeping vitality complete you can preserve the body. To keep vitality complete first requires that the body be settled. When settled, there is no desire, so vitality is complete.

By keeping energy complete you can nurture the mind. To keep energy complete first requires that the mind be clear and calm. When clear and calm, there are no thoughts, so energy is complete.

By keeping spirit complete you can return to openness. To keep spirit complete first requires that the will be sincere. When the will is sincere, body and mind combine and return to openness.

Therefore vitality, energy, and spirit are the three basic medicines; body, mind, and will are the three basic essentials.

Learning the science of spiritual immortality does not require a lot of doing; the elixir pill is just a matter of refining the three treasures of vitality, energy, and spirit. When the three treasures are combined in the central chamber, the gold pill is completed. It is easy to know, not hard to practice. What is hard to practice and hard to know is fallacious, mere deception.

The essential point in refining vitality is in the body. When the body is not agitated, "wind rises at the tiger's roar," "the dark tortoise hides away," and the basic vitality solidifies.

The essential point in refining energy is in the mind. When the mind is not agitated, "clouds rise at the dragon's howl," "the red sparrow folds its wings," and the basic energy rests.

The essential point in refining spirit is in the will. When the will does not waver, the celestial and the earthly combine, the three bases merge into one, and the spiritual embryo is complete.

The cauldron and furnace of HEAVEN and EARTH, the medicinal ingredients of WATER and FIRE, the eight trigrams, three bases, five forces, and four forms are all no more than body, mind, and will.

The consummation of complete reality is not outside of body and mind; whatever is apart from body and mind is an aberrant path. Yet even so, you should not get fixated on body or mind, for as soon as you get fixated on body or mind, you are burdened by body and mind. You must be one with their function, yet detached from their function.

"Body and mind" do not mean the illusory body and physical brain; they are the invisible body and mind. What are the invisible body and mind? "Clouds rise from the mountains, the moon is in the heart of the waves."

The "body" is the pure serene body of all time, subtle being within nonbeing. The "mind" is the root of spiritual subtlety before imagination, true nonbeing within being. Being within nonbeing is represented by the *I Ching* trigram WATER ☵, nonbeing within being is represented by the trigram FIRE ☲.

Ziyang, one of the founders of the Complete Reality path, says in his classic *Understanding Reality*, "Take the solid heart in the center of WATER ☵ and change the yin inside FIRE ☲. From this it changes into the healthy body of HEAVEN ☰. Then to lie hidden or to leap into flight is entirely up to the mind." So there can be no doubt that body and mind are the point of consummation of complete reality.

The point of spiritual alchemy is a matter of essence and life only. Anything apart from essence and life is a sidetrack. Clinging to one side is bias.

One of the founding teachers said, "Spirit is essence, energy is life." This is what I am talking about.

Refining energy is a matter of preserving the body, refining spirit is a matter of preserving the mind. When the body does not stir, "the tiger roars"; when the mind does not stir, "the dragon howls." When the tiger roars, lead goes into mercury; when the dragon howls, mercury goes into lead.

Lead and mercury are different names for WATER and FIRE. The yang ▬ in WATER ☵ is the ultimate vitality in the body; the yin ▬ ▬ in FIRE ☲ is the basic energy in the mind. To refine vitality into energy is the way to first preserve the body; to refine energy into spirit is the way to first preserve the mind.

When the body is settled, one is physically firm; when physically firm, one perfects life. When the mind is settled, the spirit is complete; when the spirit is complete, one perfects essence. When body and mind unite, essence and life are complete, and one is physically and spiritually sublimated, this is called completion of the elixir.

When vitality turns into energy and energy turns into spirit, this is not yet wonderful. Why? There is still the subtlety of refining the spirit, which is not easy to speak of.

What I have spoken of is the general outline of spiritual alchemy. If you have insight, you will believe the great matter is not on paper. Otherwise, you should know where to set to work. Once you know where to set to work, then practice accordingly, beginning with refinement of vitality. After vitality is stabilized, then refine energy. After energy is stabilized, then refine spirit. After spirit is stabilized, then return to openness. When empty and open, you are imbued with the qualities of the Tao.

Refining vitality is a matter of knowing the time. In this context, "time" does not mean terrestrial time. If you cling to terrestrial time, that is not it. But if you say there is no time, how do you set to work? The ancients said that when the time arrives the spirit knows. One of the founding teachers said, "When lead sees winter, you should hasten to gather it." These words tell all: lead is true sense, winter is utter stillness; stilling conditioned feelings allows true sense to emerge—when true sense emerges, gather it at once.

Refining energy is a matter of harmonization. Harmonization means harmonization of the true breath and the true basis. Lao-tzu said, "The door of the mysterious female is called the root of heaven and earth. Continuously there as such, using it is not forced." This is the essential point of harmonization.

The mysterious female is the mechanism of opening and closing of heaven and earth. The *I Ching* says, "Closing the door is called EARTH, opening the door is called HEAVEN; alternate closing and opening is called change." Alternating closing and opening is alternating stillness and movement. This is the meaning of Lao-tzu's statement "using it is not forced."

An alchemical text says, "Breathing out contacts the root of heaven, breathing in contacts the root of earth. On breathing out, the dragon howls, clouds arise; on breathing in, the tiger roars, wind arises." I say that "breathing out contacts the root of heaven, breathing in contacts the root of earth" is the same as "closing the door is called EARTH, opening the door is called HEAVEN." "On breathing out, the dragon howls, clouds arise; on breathing in, the tiger roars, wind arises" is the same as "the alternation of closing and opening is called change." It is also the meaning of "using it is not forced." The breathing referred to here is the endless coming and going of the true breath, the pulse of life within the cyclic changes of the macrocosm and the microcosm.

XV.

SPOKEN TEACHINGS

The functions of vitality, energy, and spirit are twofold, but their substance is one. In terms of the outer medicine, first sexual vitality must not be used compulsively. Then the energy of breath must be very subtle, until there is no noticeable breathing. Then the spirit of thought should be calm and quiet.

The coming and going of external yin and yang is the outer medicine; the combining of internal WATER and FIRE is the inner medicine. The outer involves active application, the inner is spontaneous.

The functions of vitality, energy, and spirit are twofold, but their substance is one. In terms of the outer medicine, first sexual vitality must not be used compulsively; then the energy of breath must be very subtle, until there is no noticeable breathing; then the spirit of thought should be calm and quiet.

In terms of the inner medicine, refining vitality means refining the basic vitality, taking the primordial awareness out of the mundane context. This is represented as taking the basic yang out of WATER ☵. When the basic vitality is stabilized, then sexual vitality is naturally not compulsive.

Refining energy means refining the basic energy, taking the condition-ing out of ordinary consciousness. This is represented as filling in the yin inside FIRE ☲. When the basic energy is stabilized, the energy of breath naturally does not go out and in.

Refining spirit means refining the basic spirit, combining subconscious real knowledge with conscious ordinary knowledge. This is represented as combining WATER ☵ and FIRE ☲ to make HEAVEN ☰. When the basic spirit is stabilized, the spirit of thought is at peace.

Beyond this, there is still the stage of refining spaciousness, which is not easy to speak of; it is best understood tacitly. Work on this.

XVI.

DISCOURSES

If those who cultivate life do not understand essence, how can they escape the movement of time? If those who see essence do not know life, where will they wind up in the end?

ON ESSENCE AND LIFE

"Essence" refers to the primordial, utterly inconceivable spirit. "Life" refers to the primordial, utterly vital energy. Vitality and spirit are the root of essence and life.

The development of essence relates to mind; the development of life relates to the body.

Understanding and knowledge come from the mind; with thought and imagination, the mind employs essence. Actions and reactions come from the body; with speech and silence, looking and listening, the body burdens life.

When life is burdened by the body, there is birth and death. When essence is employed by the mind, there is coming and going.

So we know body and mind are the abodes of vitality and spirit, vitality and spirit are the bases of essence and life.

Essence cannot be there without life, life cannot be there without essence. Though there are two names, in principle they are one.

It is a pity that students today—Buddhists and Taoists—divide essence and life into two, each fixated on one side. Buddhists are fixated on essence, Taoists on life; criticizing each other, they do not realize that neither solitary yin nor isolated yang can fulfill the great work.

If those who cultivate life do not understand essence, how can they escape the movement of time? If those who see essence do not know life, where will they wind up in the end?

An immortal teacher said, "Refining the gold elixir pill without realizing essence is the number one sickness of practice; but if you just cultivate the true essence and not the elixir, the yin spirit cannot enter enlightenment for myriad eons." How true these words are!

Highly developed people master both essence and life. First they open their minds by discipline, concentration, and insight; then they preserve their bodies by refining vitality, energy, and spirit.

When the vitality is settled, the foundation of life is permanently stabilized; when the mind is open and clear, the basis of essence is completely illumined.

When essence is completely illumined, there is no coming or going; when life is stabilized, there is no death or birth.

At the point of complete unification, one enters right into noncontrivance; essence and life both complete, one is physically and mentally sublimated.

Still, it cannot be said that essence and life are fundamentally two; yet they cannot be explained as one matter either. They are fundamentally one, but the function is twofold.

Those who are fixated and partial, each setting up one aspect to enter into, are those who do not understand essence and life. If you do not understand essence and life, then there is dichotomization. As long as essence and life are not preserving each other, it is impossible to attain reality.

ON THE SYMBOLISM OF THE *I CHING* SIGNS

The adept Haiqiong said that in the highest type of spiritual alchemy there are no signs or lines. So why do the alchemical books all use signs and lines from the *I Ching*? It is because all the sages set up teachings to illustrate the Tao. This is the meaning of the ancient saying, "There are no words for the Tao, but without words we cannot reveal the Tao."

The signs are like signs hung in the sky to show people something, just as nature gives signs of what bodes well and ill, so people can easily see. Symbols represent this; the lines are similitudes.

The trigram signs have three lines; these represent heaven, earth, and humanity, which are our three bases. The six lines of the hexagram signs represent the six directions of space, which are our head, feet, chest, back, and hands.

The reason why alchemical texts use the *I Ching* signs and their lines is so that students will set up the "furnace" based on the pattern of the symbols and foster the "fire" according to the lines; these provide readily accessible guidelines. The reason Haiqiong said there are no signs or lines is to warn people not to get mired in the lines and symbols, to actualize the function in a detached way.

For example, before this body is born, as-is-ness is unmoving—this is the time before the dichotomization of the absolute. Establishing essence and life based on the existence of this body is the absolute producing the two modes of yin and yang. When there are form and substance, then there are essence and sense—this is the two modes producing the four signs. Ultimately the vitality, spirit, higher soul, lower soul, will, energy, body, and mind are all complete—this is the four signs producing the eight trigrams.

A sage of old said, "Buddhists cultivate concentration in the chamber of FIRE, Taoists seek the mystery in the domain of WATER." These are said to be the essential points in refining essence and life.

Cultivating concentration in the chamber of FIRE means practicing discipline, concentration, and insight, not allowing sense objects to influence one, so that myriad existents are void. This is getting rid of the yin in the center of FIRE ☲, which means removing mundane conditioning from consciousness.

Seeking the mystery in the domain of WATER means refining vitality, energy, and spirit, causing the three flowers to assemble on the peak and the five energies to return to the source. This is keeping the yang in the center of WATER ☵, which means preserving the primordial awareness underlying the original vitality of life.

Exceptionally accomplished people master both principles, bearing yin and embracing yang, emptying the mind of compulsive conditioning and filling the being with primal energy. This is represented as taking the yang in the center of WATER and using it to fill the yin in the center of FIRE, thus producing once again the body of HEAVEN. This is what Ziyang's classic *Understanding Reality* means when it says, "Take the fullness in the center of WATER to change the yin in FIRE, thus transforming it into the whole body of HEAVEN. Then to lie hidden or to leap into flight is entirely up to the mind."

As for using the signs and lines in carrying out the firing process, in the two hexagrams HEAVEN ☰ and EARTH ☷, strength and gentility depend on each other, coming and going alternately, establishing the four seasons, making a year, with the operation of the four qualities of creativity, development, fruition, and consummation going on endlessly. The firing process, with its advance and withdrawal, extraction and addition, increasing and decreasing, is modeled on and represented by this, concentrating a year into a month, concentrating a month into a day, concentrating a day into an hour, concentrating an hour into one breath. From a world-age on the macrocosmic scale down to a single breath on the microcosmic scale, everything has a cyclic movement. Those who understand this principle get the essence of the active and passive phases of the alchemical process.

But even though spiritual alchemy uses signs and its firing process uses their lines, these are all just symbols, and you should not get fixated on the signs and lines. You should know that you may need a raft to cross a river, but you do not need a boat when you get to the other shore; when you have caught the fish, forget the net, when you have caught the rabbit, forget the trap. This is what Ziyang meant when he wrote in his *Understanding Reality*, "When you get the meaning here, stop looking for symbols; if you study the lines, you are using your mind in vain," and "Distinguish midnight and noon within unmarked time, determine HEAVEN and EARTH in lineless signs."

I say that those born knowing realize on their own without seeking, hit the mark without trying—they do not need inductive teachings, so the highest type of spiritual alchemy does not use signs and lines. Mediocre and lesser people cannot understand directly and must enter gradually; therefore the alchemical texts all use *I Ching* lines and signs as guidelines for method. Those with understanding can comprehend them by themselves through contemplation.

XVII.

EXPLANATORY TALKS

If you do not cling to appearances, appearances will not cling to you.
If you are not obsessed with anything, nothing will hold you.

DEATH AND LIFE

Lao-tzu said people think lightly of death because of their eagerness for life. He also said that only those who do not make a fuss about life are wise in terms of valuing life.

This mean that when you look for life, after all you cannot find it—then how can there be death? When there is life, then there is death; if there is no death, there is no life.

So we know that in the great matter of essence and life, death and life are important.

If you want to know death, you must first know life. When you know life, then you naturally know death. When Tzu-lu asked Confucius about death, Confucius said, "As long as you do not know life, how can you know death?" How great are the words of a sage! This seems to be what the *I Ching* means by the expression, "Find out the beginning, comprehend the end, thereby know the explanation of death and life."

I say that when those who study the Tao want to comprehend the end, they first find out the beginning; when they want to know the final end, they investigate the immediate present. If you are free right now, you will be free at the end; if you are independent right now, you will be independent at the end.

The ability of the enlightened ones of all times to shed the mundane, become spiritually transformed, and adapt to changes endlessly, comes from their having purified themselves beforehand; thus at the end they rose lightly. If people can see through all situations in everyday life and get past them, not being blinded by things, not being compelled by entanglements, then in the end nothing will be able to blind them, no emotional entanglements will be able to hold them.

I see people practicing meditation nowadays who drift into all sorts of imaginations as soon as they close their eyes. Once they have entered the realm of deception, they become one with their delusions, quite unawares. Sometimes they become aware of it, but are not able to drive delusions away. They become like zombies—they have all their ordinary sense faculties, but they are not able to use them freely; they are confused by imaginations and are unable to put them aside. Since they cannot be free right now, how can they be free on the border of life and death?

If you are stable and strong, then it will be the same whether your eyes are open or closed—you will not be affected by any illusory states. Coming and going unhindered, you will have great freedom. If you are free now, why worry about not being free at the end?

The work you do right now is itself the great matter of the end. The immediate present is the cause, the end is the result. All present thoughts lead into mundanity, all illusory reifications are in the realm of deception. If you can clear them away in ordinary life, then you will not be confused by them at the end.

Random or confused thoughts should be gotten rid of by reason, illusory reifications should be cut off by will. When thoughts end, mundanity vanishes; when illusory reifications are empty, deceptions disappear. This is how the celestial emerges. After long long practice, the mundane is exhausted and the celestial is total—this is called immortality.

When conditions increasing thoughts arise, and you let your mind follow along, then mundanity grows and deception is strong. This is how the celestial fades away. If this goes on habitually for a long long time, until the celestial is exhausted and mundanity is total, you die.

As long as any mundanity is left in those engaged in the great work, they do not become immortal; as long as any of the celestial is left in ordinary people, they do not die. Those who see this are of high rank in the mystic school.

Establish firm resolve, keep the mind free from doubt; directly bring about bare clean open clarity, not allowing any defiling attachment or fixation—then this is the pure spiritual body.

If you do not cling to appearances, appearances will not cling to you. If you are not obsessed with anything, nothing will hold you. If you do not watch anyone, no one will watch you. If you do not mind anything, nothing will mind you. If you do not focus on any sensations, no sensations will focus on you.

When sense data do not enter, the senses are pure; form, sensation, conception, conditioning, and consciousness are all empty. Then both ordinary and extraordinary perceptive capacities become complete and clear. When you reach this point, the senses perform each other's functions, and the whole body becomes an eye. Mundanities end, and the whole being is purely celestial. Essence and life are both complete, and one merges with the Tao in reality. What more death or life are there to transcend? There is no cause, no result, no combination; you reach great ease, great freedom. Herein is consummated the wonder of acquiescence in beginninglessness.

MOVEMENT AND STILLNESS

Lao-tzu said, "Effecting utter emptiness, keeping utterly still, as myriad beings act in concert, I thereby watch the return." This means movement takes place when stillness culminates. Lao-tzu goes on to say, "Beings are manifold, but each returns to the root. Returning to the root is called stillness; this means reverting to Life itself." This means that when movement culminates it reverts to stillness.

Lao-tzu also said, "Returning to Life is called the constant." This means that stillness turning to movement and movement turning to stillness is the constant of the Tao.

If movement is taken to be movement, and stillness is taken to be stillness, this is normal for beings. An ancient sage has said, "Still, yet in movement; in movement, yet still—this is spirit. Moving without stillness, still without movement—this is an ordinary being."

What is essential for preserving body and mind is not beyond movement and stillness. Students of the Tao collect body and mind, effect utter emptiness, and keep utter stillness; then they can watch return. The *I Ching* says, "Return means seeing the heart of heaven and earth."

The *I Ching* sign RETURN ☷ represents returning from EARTH ☷; that is, moving from stillness. Five yins _ _ are in the sign, standing for utter stillness; one yang __ moves below them—this is called "return." This is movement upon the culmination of stillness.

Watching return is knowing transformation; knowing transformation is not being subject to it; not being subject to transformation is returning to the root. "Returning to the root is called stillness; this means reverting to Life itself." This is reversion to stillness upon the culmination of movement.

The Connected Sayings commentary in the *I Ching* says, "Closing the door is called EARTH, opening the door is called HEAVEN. Alternate closing and opening is called change. Coming and going endlessly is called attainment." Alternate closing and opening are alternate stillness and movement; coming and going endlessly is stillness and movement unceasing. Alternating stillness and movement, the working goes on unceasingly, motivating, developing, creating, completing. This is called change. To carry this forth, adapting to changes endlessly, is called attainment.

Lao-tzu said, "The valley spirit undying is called the mysterious female." This means that when open awareness is not obscured, then the mechanism of movement and stillness cannot be inhibited. Lao-tzu also said, "The door of the mysterious female is called the root of heaven and earth." This refers to the opening and closing of the yang of HEAVEN and the yin of EARTH producing change and evolution.

Lao-tzu also said, "Continuously there as such, using it is not forced." This means the same thing as "coming and going endlessly is called attainment." The opening and closing of heaven and earth is like a person's breathing. Breathing out contacts the root of heaven; this is called opening. Breathing in contacts the root of earth; this is called closing. On breathing out, the dragon howls, clouds arise; on breathing in, the tiger roars, wind arises—this is called change. Wind and clouds meet, the dragon and tiger interact, movement and stillness depend on each other, the obvious and subtle unseparated—this is called attainment.

What I call breathing is not a matter of mouth and nose. It means the true breath coming and going continuously without ceasing, the pulse of Life, the drumming and dancing of heaven and earth.

Those who know that the change and movement of heaven and earth are the doing of spirit are called developed people. Those who comprehend this principle then realize that the power of the path of HEAVEN that does not cease is identical to the movement of one's own mind, with un-contrived work going on endlessly; and the richness of the path of EARTH that supports beings is identical to the stillness of one's own body, with function responding to things inexhaustibly.

The mind is patterned on heaven, so it is clear; the body is patterned on earth, so it is tranquil. When always clear and always tranquil, the mechanism of opening and closing of heaven and earth is one's own domain. This is what is meant by the scriptural saying, "Clarity is the source of turbidity, movement is the foundation of stillness; if people can always be clear and serene, heaven and earth will come to them."

Here I have dealt with the essential points of preserving body and mind in terms of movement and stillness. The intention is that people will collect body and mind, in the process of emulating heaven and earth. Preserving the body is a matter of harmonious attunement; preserving the mind is a matter of careful concentration.

For harmonious attunement, movement is valuable; for careful concentration, stillness is valuable. Movement is patterned on heaven, stillness is patterned on earth; when body and mind are both calm, heaven and earth join.

At the consummation of utter stillness, there is nonordinary movement of the spontaneous true potential responding inconceivably. It is precisely this mechanism of movement that is the celestial mind. Once the celestial mind is seen, the mysterious pass is penetrated; and once the mysterious pass is penetrated, the cauldron and furnace are herein, the firing process is herein, the three bases, eight trigrams, four signs, five forces, and all sorts of functions are all complete herein.

When the work reaches this point, body and mind merge, movement and stillness complement each other, and the mechanism of opening and closing of heaven and earth is entirely within oneself. Eventually the mind returns to open quiescence and the body enters nondoing; movement and stillness are both forgotten, vitality stabilizes, and energy transmutes.

At this point, vitality naturally turns into energy, energy naturally turns into spirit, and spirit naturally turns into openness, uniting with cosmic space. This is called going back to the root, returning to the origin. Here the path of everlasting life and eternal vision is completed.

XVIII.

SONGS

When emptiness is complete and open, the basic energy stabilizes;
with serenity in the midst of stillness, the celestial comes back.

On Finding Out the Tao

If mystics go through the mystic pass,
It is not hard to ascend through experience to reality.
But this minute aperture confuses people,
So they are as though separated from it by myriad mountains.
There may be alchemists in the world,
But most of them are literalists and cling to things.
Even those who struggle with the teachings
Are still like a stupid cat staying in an empty den.
Some take minerals for the matrix of the elixir,
Some say the mouth and nose are the mystic female,
Some say the heart and genitals are fire and water,
Some say blood and semen are yin and yang—
Wearying and torturing the body, wasting vitality and spirit,
They stray from the subtle basis and fail to develop.
Even when the spiritual spring is exhausted,
They still cling, unregenerate.
Everyone naturally has what's essential for immortality;
The rule of Tao obeys humanity, but humanity is unworthy—

Illusions confuse them, who looks within?
Delusions control their feelings, who reflects back?
As I see real adepts,
They penetrate both Taoism and Buddhism
And shed the constraints of attachment to religious forms;
They have the courage to withdraw from worldly ambitions
To seek the hidden Way.
It is to such sympathetic friends
That I divulge the celestial mechanism.

The primordial true awareness
Should be brought to the center of consciousness.
When a statement of the mind of Tao
Is spoken to the wise,
There is no more need for arbitrary speculation.
At the peak of illumination, watch the mind absorb vitality;
Clearly the celestial intent reveals truth.
When you understand this mechanism,
You know how to gather medicine:
When primal consciousness emerges from stillness, foster it;
In a while concentrated sense will reveal essence—
Myriad energies all arrive, and there is true bliss.
Take the reflection of truth in the world
And store it in the mind;
With active effort and detached attention,
When the power of the work arrives
It produces being within nonbeing,
Crystallizing the mystic pearl.
Yet getting the mystic pearl is still not the marvel;
Tuning the spirit and nurturing it is still more profound.
If the body is agitated or the mind is volatile,
There may be an excess of craving or irritation.
In the firing cycle, you must recognize when enough is enough;
Still and settle the three bases, and the great treasure develops.

Breaking out of the top of the head, the spirit goes free—
Then we'll walk together
To visit the abodes of immortals.

On Cultivating Openness

The Tao is fundamentally utterly open;
Open nonreification produces energy,
One energy divides into two modes:
The one above, clear, is called heaven;
The one below, opaque, is called earth.
Heaven is round and moving;
The north star, never shifting, governs motion.
Earth is square and still;
The eastward flow, never exhausted, governs stillness.
The "north star" is the heart of heaven and earth,
The "eastward flow" is the energy of heaven and earth.
When the heart is nurtured by openness,
It thereby becomes still;
When energy is nurtured by openness,
It thereby circulates.
When the human mind is calm and quiet,
Like the north star not shifting,
The spirit is most open and aware.
For one who sees this
The celestial Tao is within oneself.
Then one is physically and mentally sublimated,
And cannot be compelled to change by yin and yang,
Thus transcending the process of creation.

So we know openness
Is the substance of the great Tao,
The beginning of heaven and earth:
Movement and stillness come from this,

Yin and yang operate through this,
Myriad beings are born from this.

So openness is the great root of the world.
This may be symbolized by bamboo:
Dealing with events directly,
Dealing with the world adaptably,
Managing the mind with flexibility,
Managing the body with calmness—
This is like the resilient strength of bamboo.
Forgetting emotions in action,
Forgetting thoughts in stillness,
Forgetting self in dealing with events,
Forgetting things in adapting to change—
This is like the inner emptiness of bamboo.
Establishing certain resolve,
Keeping the mind free from doubt,
Completely pervading inside and out,
Unchanging beginning to end—
This is like the endurance of bamboo.
Widely calling on adepts,
Visiting enlightened teachers everywhere,
Extending hospitality to religious mendicants,
Synthesizing Taoism, Buddhism, and Confucianism—
This is like the clustering of bamboo.
Add to this seeing the basic, embracing the fundamental,
Minimizing selfishness and desire,
Tuning the breath, exercising sincerity,
Observing transformation, knowing return—
Who can do this unless utterly open?

Taoism, Buddhism, Confucianism—
All simply transmit one openness.
Throughout all time, those who have transcended

Have done the work from within openness.
Openness and sincerity are the essence of alchemy,
Learning Buddhism is meditation plunging into openness;
And as for learning the affairs of Confucian sages,
Selflessness in openness clarifies the celestial design.

The substance of Tao, open emptiness,
Is infinitely subtle;
With HEAVEN and EARTH operating in openness,
Energy is whole and fluid.
The creation and transformation of yin and yang
Alternate in openness.
If people plunge into openness,
They will comprehend successful adaptation.

The miracle of the restorative elixir
Is in setting to work
In the valley of open nonreification,
To effect utter emptiness
And keep utter stillness.
When emptiness is complete and open,
The basic energy stabilizes;
With serenity in the midst of stillness,
The celestial comes back.
Emptying the mind, filling the middle,
Is the formulation of the path;
When you don't obscure open awareness,
That is the time for gathering the medicine.
Emptying oneself and responding to situations
Is true ordinary activity;
Union with cosmic space is greatness.

Gathering real knowledge in open serenity
Is done without contrivance;

Promoting the fire of consciousness
Is done with openness as the bellows.
Extracting and adding,
Increasing and decreasing,
All depend on openness;
Upon shattering space,
One attains great awakening.

Ultimately the Tao is applied with gentility:
Shedding superficialities
And breaking down excess intensity
Must be practiced together;
Harmonizing enlightenment to mix with the world,
One forgets others and self.

That which is prior to the reign of images
Can only be known intuitively—
How can there be symbols without signs?
HEAVEN is not above, EARTH is not below;
In the middle is a point of pure awareness.
Crystal clear on all sides, there is no gap;
Thoroughly solid in all respects,
It is completely whole:
This is the door of the mysterious female,
Open in the center.

If you act in nonempty openness,
Opening and closing will spontaneously accord
With HEAVEN and EARTH.
When the door of the mysterious female opens,
The work is consummated;
The spirit goes out through here,
And also comes in through here.
Going out again and again,

Coming in again and again,
Returning to openness,
From equanimous calm, energy bursts forth.
When energy goes into action,
Heaven and earth open,
And from openness springs forth
A sphere of brilliant light,
Shining without lack or excess.

Responding to the time and people,
One rests the spirit in openness,
Acts in openness,
Reveals the state of openness in speech.
When openness reaches the point
Where there is not even any "openness,"
Then all logic ends.
When you plunge into openness,
Heaven and earth come to you.
With open heart and upright bearing,
Be like the green bamboo;
This is the foremost device
For cultivating openness.

Breaking Up Confusion

Worldly alchemists are lamentable—
There are many different types.
Clinging to symbols literally,
Performing practices randomly,
They waste their strength
On superficialities and spin-offs.

Taking in sunlight, sipping moonlight,
Absorbing light, drinking air and fog,

Practicing various contortions,
Rolling and massaging the eyes,
Swallowing large quantities of saliva,
Pressing the coccyx and midspine,
Concentrating on imagination and sustaining thoughts,
Staring at the tip of the nose,
Ingesting feces and urine,
Maintaining quietistic aloofness,
Falling into indifferent emptiness,
Practicing impulsively, now still, now active,
Practicing massage and counting breaths—
All of these are different
From the principle of the gold pill.

Calisthenics, six-sound breathing, avoiding grains—
What do these accomplish?
Obsession with sexual practices to gather yin,
Considering "nine shallow strokes, one deep"
To be "advancing and withdrawing,"
Relaxing the waist and cupping the testicles in the hand
To "protect the door of life,"
Bending and stretching to circulate energy,
Performing mental gymnastics,
Strengthening military arts—
Schools such as this
Are not worth talking about.

Then there are those who hold their breath,
Stretch like a bear
And contract their limbs like birds,
Causing useless strain.
Devotees who massage their waists
Are warm in the belly;
Practitioners who circulate breath
Are red in the face.

Tapping the back of the head,
Cradling the skull in the arms,
Chattering the teeth to "gather the spirits,"
Gazing at the top of the head—
Empty echoes are taken to be
The roar of the male tiger,
Rumbling in the belly is said to be
The howl of the female dragon.
Warming the lower abdomen
Adjusts a boiling sea;
Those who go sleepless day and night
Struggle to keep their eyes open.
Wearing a single robe, going barefoot,
Suffering from burning heat,
Lack in past life
Is paid back by hunger and cold.

Continually not talking is idle vanity;
How can one ascend to immortality
By silently paying court to the lord on high?
Sporting the "golden lance,"
Holding up the "golden well,"
Taking a beautiful woman as the cauldron of the elixir,
Calling sexual fluids the true lead—
Losing original harmony, they are still unaware.

Some babble on about Zen,
Loquaciously showing off their ability to speak;
Pointing to the sky, they talk of voidness,
Making a useless fuss.
Raising a fist, holding up a finger,
They do not know the source;
Bringing up sayings and contemplative methods,
They quip and jabber.
They deal with students by picking up a gavel,

Or by holding up a whisk;
Winking the eyes and raising the eyebrows
They consider awakening.
They consider studying stories
To be pure concentration.
A genuine highly developed Buddhist
Is never like those
Who consider rationalization wisdom,
Who will never clarify the mind
Or see its essence.

Taoist, Confucian, Buddhist—stop clinging!
Turn the attention inward to illumine within,
Think for yourself.
Suddenly you will find your nose is pointed,
And then you will finally realize
That you have been wrong all along.

Students of immortality—stop discussion,
Find out the basis of initial reception of energy.
Formalities and reified quests do not stand;
Have no more to do with formlessness either.

The heart is not fire, the genitals not water;
Ordinary vitality cannot be called the natural vitality.
The yellow woman is not in the spleen;
Stop saying the mysterious female is in the mouth and nose.
Six a.m. is not the rabbit,
Six p.m. is not the rooster;
Midnight is not water, noon is not fire.
The first yang is not in numbers,
Keeping full is not fixed to the time of the full moon.
The liver is not the dragon, the lungs not the tiger;
How can sexual fluids be called the matrix of the elixir?

The five forces are basically just one yin and yang,
The four signs are not apart from the dual mysterious female.
The river source where medicine is gathered
Is not easy to know;
Essence is always within oneself,
Sense has to be recovered from externals.
In the abode of consciousness,
The higher soul, the solar soul, is the "girl";
In the abode of vitality,
The lower soul, the lunar soul, is the "boy."

Doing or nondoing,
Studying or not studying,
Self-centered practitioners
Are all in an ivory tower.

Now I reveal the device
Completely in one statement:
Body and mind are the fire and medicine;
When body and mind are stable and settled,
The mystic teaching is mastered;
Vitality, energy, and spirit
Merge in open spontaneity.
In three hundred days,
The embryonic spirit is released;
Turning about,
One shatters cosmic space.

On the Mystic Principle

Though the supreme Tao has no location,
Still it is necessary that an adept transmit guidelines.
Effort and innocence are symbolically associated
With morning and evening;

Transitions from stillness to movement and movement to stillness
Are provisionally labeled midnight and noon.
Promoting the fire is refining the great elixir
Within nonreification;
Settling the furnace is seeking the true will
Within concentration.
When body, mind, and will are settled,
They join the three sets:
Sense and vitality,
Essence and spirit,
Together with will—
All have the same ancestor.
Increasing the celestial and reducing the mundane
According to the time,
There is an orderly process.
Guarding the castle is in oneself
Distinguishing host and guest.
Essence is in the mind,
Sense is in the body:
When the two medicinal ingredients merge,
Vitality and energy flow into and out of one another.

Directly transcending to ultimate reality,
One betakes oneself to the Great Vehicle.
Immediate understanding with complete pervasion
Is no small boon;
Inner understanding of the true potential
Is basically spontaneous.

Pitiful are the petty techniques upheld at random;
The glib of tongue boast of their abilities.
Who can even look at them
In their vanity and conceit?
They do not know how to plunge their minds
Into profound abstraction—

Why should they bother to set goals
And live in sanctuaries?
Beginners who do not seek teachers
Grow old without attainment,
Bringing misery upon themselves.

Accumulate accomplishments and deeds,
Be of service to humanity.
Turn the attention inward as well
To find receptivity and creativity.
Rouse the awareness within,
And the tiger roars wind;
Wash away dust from the senses,
And the dragon makes rain.
Action and illumination need the polar star
Of constant, unwavering insight;
Fostering the true and removing the false
Is up to stillness, the warrior of darkness.
By the time conscious essence
Comes from the abode of spirit,
The sense of reality has already reached
The abode of vitality.
When one pill of the great elixir
Forms in the furnace,
The embryonic immortal in the room
Dances three leaps.
The four signs and five energies
All combine harmoniously,
The nine-restoration and seven-reversion
Complete the work cycle.
The radiant form of the moon appears from the hut,
The shining light illumines the universe.

In governing human affairs
And serving the celestial,

It is best to be sparing;
This is called piling up virtue.
Too much introspection into the sky of essence
Increases defilement of sense;
Too much reasoning
Increases habituated consciousness.
Intellectual brilliance is not as good
As being simpleminded;
Eloquence and lofty talk
Are not as good as silence.
Cutting off rumination, forgetting impulses,
Then there are no judgments;
Hiding one's light,
Keeping one's development concealed,
One is aloof from sound and form.
When desire and taste are minimized,
Basic goodness arrives;
When affairs are reduced, involvements simplified,
The root of virtue is planted.

In a moment of perfect fluidity,
Myriad thoughts are cleared;
Passing through mundane and transmundane mindfulness,
All entanglements cease.
On careful examination of the writings
Of the sages of the three teachings,
I find the word "stopping"
Most simple and direct.
If you can work on the basis of stopping,
It will not be hard to become an enlightened wizard.
Stopping entanglements and arriving at the source
Is the mechanism of Chan Buddhism;
Stopping the mind and clarifying noumenon
Is the consummation of Confucianism;

Stopping energy and stabilizing spirit
Is the mystery of Taoism.
These three stoppings
Are interdependent, overcoming all;
To thoroughly investigate your own mind
Is the guiding principle.

The Inner Design of Essence

When the two modes first differentiate,
They distinguish three poles:
HEAVEN is focused on directness,
EARTH opens and closes;
Between heaven and earth,
The door of the mysterious female—
In its movement is increasing outflow,
In its stillness, increasing penetration.
The accurate transmission
Of the guiding basis of Tao
Points the way to the ultimate.

Sense goes with the body,
Essence goes with the mind;
Energy fosters awareness,
Vitality nurtures life.
In eliciting knowledge
By investigating phenomena,
There are typical constants;
On entering sagehood,
Transcending the ordinary,
There are no longer ranks.
Developed people live in the midst of change,
Awaiting the direction of Life;
Inwardly aware, unafflicted,

What worry is there?
Effecting function, promoting illumination,
Is the mechanism of enlivening freedom
And killing slavery to compulsion:
Remembering the ultimate end of the body,
Volatility and aggression disappear.
Turning the attention around,
You see through the dream body
And directly throw over
The raft of ancient books.

Polish the light, remove accretions,
Dissolve accumulated burdens,
Clarify the mind,
Be free of addictive habituation.
Submerge the mind in the subtle,
Sense and penetrate;
You will drink an endless river
In a single gulp.

No need to refine the essence of gold
In the crucible of HEAVEN,
Or cook jade broth
On the stove of EARTH—
On passing through, penetrating
Before the creation of symbols,
The world, when taken in,
Lies hidden in a tiny grain.

The Firing Process

If you want to reach the mystery of mysteries,
You need to be careful when alone.
The mechanism of the work is in the eye:

Cut off the dust of form
And you will be impeccable;
The clear open heart
Will shine like jade.

Bring about utter emptiness,
Keep stillness steady;
Within stillness, a moving yang of creative energy returns.
At the first yang, the hidden dragon should be under control;
Then when you get to seeing the dragon, do not be hasty.
As soon as you experience "working hard," light illumines within;
When "sometimes leaping, in the abyss," then bathe.
At the fifth yang, the flying dragon
Effects evolution and development.
Then when yang peaks, yin arises,
Necessitating withdrawal, preventing insidious inroads.

At the first yin of EARTH,
Withdraw to where sense joins essence.
At the third yin, "it won't do to glorify with emolument."
After "closing the bag," the spiritual elixir is ripe;
If you meet with "battle in the field,"
Set your will on locking up tight.

When the mundane is stripped away
And the celestial is pure,
Then the firing is sufficient;
A tiny pearl is swallowed into the belly,
Producing a complete real member of the immortals.
Yin and yang are always in harmony,
Their combinations proportionate
In accordance with the time.
Essence and sense live together,
Conscious knowledge and real knowledge spontaneously join.

Having finished making space into an unconstructed abode,
This host is truly no ordinary worldling.
The mountain crags hiding the clouds,
Heaven and earth are clear;
The shining light of the moon
Illumines the open valley.

The Dragon and the Tiger

PREFACE

Dragon and tiger are different names for yin and yang; the process of yin and yang is sublimely subtle, unfathomable, so it is symbolized by the dragon and tiger.

The Connected Sayings in the *I Ching* say, "One yin, one yang—this is called Tao. The unfathomability of yin and yang is called spiritual." Alchemical literature says, "Unbalanced yin and unbalanced yang are called illnesses."

Yin and yang are the stillness and movement of the absolute. The One divides into two, the clear rises while the opaque sinks. Both the macrocosm and all microcosms have forms and descriptions due to the two energies of yin and yang. Therefore there is nothing in the world, large or small, that is outside yin and yang.

The various different names in the alchemical classics and writings of the adepts all refer only to yin and yang. Generations of immortality teachers, borrowing names to set up images, have symbolized yin and yang as a dragon and a tiger. This was to enable students to get an easy grip on the pattern whereby to accomplish the work.

The image of dragon and tiger is that of countless changes and transformations, marvelous subtlety difficult to comprehend. Therefore they are called medicinal substances. When speaking in terms of "setting up," they are referred to as the cauldron and furnace; when speaking in terms of being "put into operation," they are referred to as the firing process. They are compared to WATER and FIRE, represented as wood and metal, named woman and man, paired as wife and husband.

All of these different terms refer to subtle functions of the dragon and tiger. Because of their miraculous effect, they are called medicinal substances. Because they make things, they are called cauldron and furnace. Because they transmute, they are called the firing process. Because they interact for balance, they are called WATER and FIRE. Because they are straight and firm, they are called wood and metal. Because of their subtle communion, they are called wife and husband. What else but dragon and tiger could comprehend all this?

A literary work says, "Clouds follow a dragon, wind follows a tiger; sages create, while all beings watch." This illustrates the quality of creative origination, which is represented by the fifth yang in the hexagram HEAVEN. We know that the subtlety of the dragon and tiger cannot be attained but for the spiritual qualities and the accomplishments of sages.

When you look for the dragon and tiger in yourself, they are essence and sense; transmuted and adjusted, they are mind and body, higher and lower souls, spirit and vitality. Carry them forth in action, and they are the door of the mysterious female, the mechanism of opening and closing.

Lao-tzu said, "The valley spirit not dying is called the mysterious female. The door of the mysterious female is called the root of heaven and earth. Continuously there as such, using it is not forced."

The I Ching says, "Closing the door is called EARTH, opening the door is called HEAVEN; one closing, one opening—this is called change. Coming and going endlessly is called attainment."

An alchemical text says, "Breathing out, you touch the root of heaven; breathing in, you touch the root of earth." This is the mechanism of opening and closing. "When you breathe out, the dragon bellows, clouds arise; when you breathe in, the tiger roars, wind arises." This is opening and closing referred to as change. "Wind and clouds sense each other and combine, producing gold liquid." This is coming and going endlessly referred to as attainment.

When the "gold liquid" of spiritual energy is restored, it crystallizes into the great elixir pill. Therefore the pill is provisionally labeled the great dragon-tiger pill. Take it and you will live long and see forever.

The breathing referred to here is not ordinary respiration; it is the door of exit and entry of the subtle interactions of the real potential.

If you actually penetrate through here, the dragon-tiger pill is completed, and there is hope for spiritual immortality. If true cultivators of reality can really gain lucid, penetrating understanding of the dragon and tiger, even though the real eternal Tao is said to be most mysterious and subtle, still it can be attained.

As for the matter of performing worthwhile actions to nurture the embryo of enlightenment, there are none that are accomplished without understanding the dragon and tiger.

The adept Ziyang said collecting body and mind is called conquering the dragon and subduing the tiger. When the mind does not move, the dragon bellows; when the body does not move, the tiger roars. When the dragon bellows, the energy is stabilized; when the tiger roars, the vitality is solidified.

When the basic vitality is solidified, this is sufficient to preserve the physical. When the basic energy is stabilized, this is sufficient to solidify the spiritual. Physically and spiritually sublimated, merging in reality with the Tao, the task of spiritual immortality is done.

Zhao Shu-zai was a courtier when he was young, and served in middle-level official capacities. Through the revolving of heaven and earth he saw through the evanescent life, so he gave up ambition and took to seeking the essence of the Tao. Though he lives in the ordinary world, in reality his mind rests in the mystic realm, and he is actually one who has shed the burden of worldly affairs.

Wishing to unify and solidify the spirit, he has therefore been concentrating on the dragon and tiger. One day he brought a diagram to show me, and asked me to add some words. I could not refuse, so I have written this to satisfy his request.

I said to him, "The ancients set up images based on the Tao; now I have set up words based on images. It is important to exercise clear perception and see through to the real point. Do not make the mistake of sticking to the zero point of the scale. If you can understand the meaning through words, and get the message by contemplating diagrams, then you know the real dragon and tiger are not on paper, but in oneself. When words and images are both forgotten, the qualities of Tao are all there.

"Yes, the real dragon and real tiger are not hard to seek—it just requires using yang to complement yin. Then the four qualities of origination, development, fruition, and consummation operate, powerful, true, and unceasing; hidden, flying, appearing, leaping—it is all up to the mind. But even so, this is still rousing waves on even ground, thunder in a clear sky. Work on this."

THE SONG

The real dragon and real tiger
Originally have no image—
Who can create a model of them
To convey what they are like?

If you understand them in formlessness,
You still fall into extremism
And wind up dissolute.
It is so clear,
Clear as the sun in the blue sky—
But even this is making waves
Where there is no wind.

If people now want to know,
The real dragon and tiger
Are not in the province of being or nonbeing,
Or the realm of midnight or noon.

Don't swallow the two things mixed up;
Just count the five forces backward.
The root and stem are originally
The chamber of utter mystery;
Creative evolution is in the crimson hill mansion,
The abode of the primordial vitality.

Though application involves deliberate conscious extension,
Ultimately open awareness has no fixed locus.
The unique universal Tao requires mental penetration;
The minute spiritual working is not visible to the eye.
When it suddenly bursts out
And opens the top of your head,
You see that sense and essence
Have the same one mother.

On the loftiest heights the celestial mind
Surveys all around;
The dipper of precise attention
Draws from the silver river of energy.

Congealing energy depends on concentration;
Insight and action emerge from profound stillness.
In a flash the celestial and the earthly commune;
Instantly reason and desire complement one another.

The tiger produces a clear sense of real knowledge,
The dragon showers the sweet rain of conscious essence:
Clouds roll, rain enriches, all the world is at peace—
Operating the creative dragon power, the work is completed.

People say heaven can be brought under control
By six dragons—
Who knows one dragon is the true host?
People say that five tigers
Get through the mysterious pass—
Who knows one tiger produces real will?

When you understand the normal harmony
Of the association of the dragon and tiger,

Then you know the tortoise and snake of energy and vitality
Swallow and spit out one another.

Sages set up symbols as a means to point to traces;
Understand outside of symbols, and you get to the mystical.
You must find the intent of adepts outside words;
Originally the absolute has no sphere.
To forget the symbol once you get the idea is still nothing special;
Forgetting even the idea is the ultimate rule.

Nothingness and Oneness

The Tao, basically open and nonreified,
Produces the absolute:
The absolute changes and there is the first one;
One divides into two, two produce three,
And the four signs and five forces emerge from here.

The nonreified One is the root of heaven and earth;
In the mystic teaching, One is the door of all subtleties.
The *I Ching* distinguishes creation and evolution from within One,
The human mind employs general norms on the basis of One.

When heaven attains oneness it is clear,
When earth attains oneness it is peaceful;
A valley is thereby filled,
Spirit is thereby aware.
Things are made by it,
Humans are born from it;
If leaders and rulers get it,
The country is secure.

Chan transmits true guidance within One,
Confucianism distinguishes opening and closing from One,

Taoism expounds true eternity by means of One.
The Confucian "Unique One" is immeasurably subtle;
Taoism has three vehicles, Chan has five branches:
Ultimately a thousand lamps are all one light.

Embrace the fundamental, preserve oneness,
Go through the mystic opening;
Thoroughly unified, understand
The teaching of sages.

The great mystery, the real One,
Is the gateway to restoration of Life;
So we know that the One
Is the real eternal Way.

Stop saying when One is attained everything is done;
Attaining oneness, keep One, preserve it without loss.
Once you penetrate, all merges,
And the celestial design is clear.

All phenomena are ultimately one,
But this is still nothing extraordinary;
The beginning is one Nonbeing,
Which produces all beings.
With nonbeing and being working together,
It is possible to last long.

If you can really return all to One, without partner,
You will know how to face south to see the north star.
When you attain this, you gain oneness
And then forget the One:
Now you can appear and disappear
The same as the basis of creation.

If you cling to One and can't forget it,
You're like a stupid cat staying in an empty cave.
When the three fives merge into one,
The one returns to emptiness.
After returning to emptiness,
There isn't even any emptiness.
With even nonbeing nonexistent,
There is profound tranquility.

People today call nothingness nothing,
And as dissolute nihilists get into dreadful ways.
People today call oneness one,
And with biased clinging waste effort.

When you understand nothingness that is not nothing,
Then in preserving oneness you'll know there is no One.
When One and Nothing are both overturned,
The great task of nothingness and oneness is done.

On Embracing Unity

When the Infinite culminates
It becomes the Absolute;
Circulation of the Absolute's subtlety
Begins in the One.

The One divides into two,
Producing yin and yang;
Myriad species, heaven, earth, and humans,
All emerge from here.

Originally the true One
Is utterly open, aware;

There is no change
Throughout all time.

But due to becoming substance,
Spirit emanates cognition,
Differentiating circumstances
Into good and bad.

Following feelings pursuing illusions
Increases suffering;
Fragrance, flavor, form and sound—
All dazzle and confuse.

If you can truly find
The root source in the One,
You return to the origin,
Go back to the fundamental,
Without wasting effort.

Yin and yang commune in concentration;
Their combinations are gotten in nothingness.
The three bases and eight trigrams join in the will;
The four signs and five forces return to utter quiescence.
Suddenly bursting forth through the top of the head,
A brilliant gold light fills the spiritual room.

The valley of open nonreification
Is spontaneously cleared;
The door of the mysterious female
Opens and closes itself.

The wonder of the return of the celestial
Can never be exhausted;

The four qualities of creativity
Never ever cease.

Extending the energy
and stabilizing the spirit
In deep abstraction
Going from being into nonbeing
In a state of ecstasy,
What is the ruler within?
It is the original purpose
Of arriving at one's aim.

The Sword of Wisdom

Ever since adepts handed on
The secret of the sword,
The true imperative has been upheld
Completely, truly adamant.

If someone asks me about
Looking for its origin,
I say it is not ordinary iron.
This lump of iron
Comes from receptive stillness;
When you obtain it, it rises up.

Forging it in a glowing fire,
Through repeated efforts
It is refined
And forged into steel.

When students of the Tao
Know this secret,

The spirit of light is intensely powerful,
And devils of darkness vanish.

The subtle function of spiritual work
Is truly hard to measure;
I now give an explanation for you.
In telling you about it,
I divulge the celestial mechanism.

Setting to work when one yang comes back,
First have the six yangs pump the furnace bellows;
Then the six yins work the tongs and hammer.
When the work of firing is complete,
It produces the sword;
When it is first done,
It flashes like lightning.

Brandish it horizontally
And a cold clear breeze arises;
Hold it upright,
And the shining bright moon appears.
When the bright moon appears,
Auspicious light illumines heaven and earth;
Sprites and ghosts are distressed.

It stops turbidity, brings out clarity,
Sweeps away weird defilements;
It slays volatility,
Cuts down aggressiveness,
Destroys monsters:
Influences draining away
Vitality, energy, and spirit
All vanish in the light of the sword.

Entanglements cut off, rumination dies down,
And the web of feelings is rent asunder.
Where the spiritual edge is aimed, mountains crumble;
The demon kings of mundane planes are all routed.

This precious sword fundamentally has no form;
The name is set up because it has spiritual effect.
Learning the Tao and practicing reality
Depend on this sword;
Without this sword,
The Tao cannot be achieved.

Opening up the vast darkness,
Distinguishing heaven and earth,
Dissolving obstructions, transmuting objects—
All is included.
If you ask me to show it to you,
I bring it out before you—
Do you understand or not?

Drawing Back from Error to Truth

The Tao produces one energy
From open nonreification;
Who affixes labels,
Distinguishing phases of formation?

The one energy dichotomizes,
Producing two modes;
The clear rises, the opaque sinks,
Forming sky and earth.

The warp and woof of yin and yang
Is like a working shuttle;

The opening and closing of HEAVEN and EARTH
Is like a pumping bellows.

With the subtle combining of the two modes
There are the three components;
Seven apertures open,
Producing myriad species.

The infinite reality is a single whole,
Always present in daily activities;
Creation after creation,
Transformation after transformation,
Hundreds and thousands of workings—
None of them are beyond
This present mortal being.

If you can truly plumb
The root source by yourself,
The four signs and five forces
Are inherently complete within you.

Introspecting thrice day and night,
The will is undivided;
In the single source of eliminating materialism,
Accomplishment is multiplied a hundredfold.

Getting through the pass of vitality
And then the pass of energy,
One gains occult communication
With the pipes of heaven and earth.

In the groove everywhere,
One has guidance;

Every opening illumined,
There is no suffocating obstruction.

If you can perceive this,
You then make two faces into one die:
Raising your head,
You knock over the polar mountain;
Taking a step, you overturn
The blockade of the mystic wonder.

The unique design, simply evoked,
Expresses the true source;
It harmoniously combines myriad differences,
Resolving them in correct alignment.

Having refined the luminous spirit,
Emanate this spirit of light;
Transcend from the realm of form
Into the formless realm.

I see many practitioners today concocting wonders;
Arrogant and presumptuous, they show off and boast,
Claiming to have understanding.

A sharp wit and glib tongue
Are artificial brilliance;
Domineering talk of voidness
Is useless intellection.

Beginners are subject to deception;
Learned mystics are not liked.

Those who just show off strength for now
Are heedless of their final destruction;

Those who talk a lot in front of others
Are like selling water by a riverside.
Producing smoke and fire,
Their thoughts are off;
Pursuing objects, following fashions,
Their minds are narrow.

Toiling frantically at religious exercises,
They struggle madly to circulate vitality and energy;
Counting their breaths and massaging themselves,
They vainly aim for pleasant sensations.

Sinking into torpor,
Or rising in excitement,
They cannot extend attention;
Now torpid, now distracted,
What can be done?

When the spirit wanes away
And the energy dissipates,
How can this be cured?
When the body is exhausted,
Regret is useless.

If you see the straight path
Out of confusion,
To escape the burden of payment
Of the debt of harmful practices,
Then collect your scattered mind
And overturn your arrogant attitude.

Extend familial duty to serving teachers;
To get the teaching, first maintain discipline.

Extend sympathy for yourself to sympathy for all;
Not attacking or blaming others is based on generosity.

Without illuminating yourself,
You make your illumination complete;
Without aggrandizing yourself,
You make your greatness complete.

With no problems,
No cravings, no concerns,
Get rid of extremes,
Get rid of both arrogance and fawning.

To work on setting up the foundation
Requires strict discipline;
Carry out further refinement
In encounter with situations.

Use the sense of real knowledge
And the essence of conscious knowledge
To make the elixir pill;
Don't take mud for jewels.

Don't get mired in solipsism,
And don't think it's a matter
Of intellectual knowledge
Or learned understanding.

Raising a child within ultimate nonreification,
When the heaven of meditation
Is completely purified,
There's not the slightest wisp.

The mechanism of nine-restoration and seven-reversion
Is not inside and not outside:

The original nature of reality is ultimately formless;
The eternal open awareness is never obscured.

Embrace the basic, keep to the One, store it in openness;
Practice this seriously and diligently, don't be lazy.
Combine the four signs, unite the three bases;
Assemble the five forces, join the eight trigrams.

Cooking in the beginning
Of movement of positive energy,
Refining at the culmination,
There's extraction and addition;
Know when to proceed actively,
And when to withdraw into passivity.

Profoundly calm in open nonreification,
Operate the mechanism;
Deeply absorbed in ecstasy,
Spin the process of creation.

When the two medicinal ingredients
Enter the central chamber,
One stream of golden light
Illumines the four quarters.

The essence of consciousness
And the sense of reality
Are united by the go-between
Of the true and steady will.

Yin and yang join together,
Wife and husband in blissful union;
Like rain and clouds,
They forget day and night.

Energy stabilizes, vitality congeals,
Forming the spiritual embryo.

On producing the mystic pearl,
There is great amazement;
The four directions all at once
Are pervaded with great light.

Crystal clear everywhere,
Without seams or gaps,
All is one round sphere
Which no amount of money can buy.

I bow my head to students of Complete Reality;
Remember what I say—
If you will take this up directly,
It is the bridle to take hold of.

When the bridle of speech
Is put into practice, what then?
The true human without fixation
Rides upon a crane.

XIX.

POEMS

Sense must be recovered, essence is always there.

VERSES ON MEDITATION WORK

Opening Up Darkness

To restore the primal wholeness of the mind,
One must know how to remain unmoved and innocent
In spite of personal desires.
Stabilization of consciousness
Depends on a calm and steady will,
While enhancing awareness
Requires receptivity and docility.
Through attraction to truth
Combined with appropriate action,
Extraordinary consciousness
And ordinary consciousness are joined.
When inner sense of the essence of mind
Is kept in the center of attention,
With psychophysical vitality
And spiritual awareness
Yoked by unified concentration,

Then one is able to proceed by oneself
In the process of development.

Gathering Medicine

The timing involved in purifying consciousness
In order to clarify real knowledge
Is not a matter of terrestrial time;
It is to be discovered in oneself by concentration.
When the mind is not fixated
On external objects or internal impulses,
There is an access of energy,
Registered in inner awareness.
When emotions are inactive,
One can sense the essence of mind;
When generative energy is not dissipated,
Desire becomes a fuel for awareness,
And consciousness is stabilized by objectivity.
After combining intuitive and rational awareness,
And joining visceral and intellectual consciousness,
When mundane conditioning loses its command
And primal conscious energy is freed from adulteration,
Then it is possible to realize objective reality.

Promoting the Fire

Having gone through the time
Of the first arising of natural energy,
You naturally have true positivity
Returning according to the time.
The fire of concentration
Emerges from the heart;
A peal of thunder along with movement
Comes from within stillness.
Energy and spirit combining

Produce spiritual substance;
Mind and breath resting on each other
Form the spiritual embryo.
When you have passed through
The experience herein,
The nine apertures
Of the three passes all open.

Daily Activity

The sense of real knowledge
And the essence of conscious knowledge
Constitute the great elixir;
These are to be gathered in formlessness.
With doing and contrivance,
After all there's cogitation;
With no seeking or grasping,
There is no worry.
Ever clear, ever calm.
The mind pearl appears;
Forgetting objects, forgetting impulses,
The jewel of life's complete.
The two roads of movement and stillness
Free from obstruction,
The isle of immortals
Is right where you are.

Stabilizing the Body

The sublime principle of Complete Reality
Is not hard to practice;
Just avoid pursuing things,
Chasing sound and form.
When illusions do not invade you,
Feelings naturally end;
When the unified mind is unaffected,

How can thoughts arise?
Get rid of discrimination of others and self,
Preserve the celestial design;
Take yin and yang in hand,
Join tranquility and development.
I tell the eminent people
Who cultivate the elixir,
When you don't indulge in the senses,
The essence is complete and clear.

Combining Yin and Yang

To reach the Tao is basically not hard;
The work lies in concentration.
When yin and yang, above and below,
Always rise and descend,
The ubiquitous flow of vital sense
Naturally returns of itself.
At the peak of awareness,
Reality becomes accessible to consciousness;
In recondite abstraction,
Nondoing joins with doing.
When the clouds recede and the rain disperses,
The spiritual embryo is complete;
The creative principle comes into play,
Producing a new birth.

Passing Through the Barrier

After all, what's the difficulty
In the real eternal Tao?
It is simply in the daily activities
Of the present time.
Once you join action and calmness
And know how to open and close,
The twin orbs of creativity and receptivity

Revolve on their own.
There is an opening
For return to the root;
There is a pass
For restoration of Life:
Having gone through these two experiences,
One transcends the ordinary,
Goes beyond the holy,
And is as if set free.

Going Out and In

The valley spirit not dying
Is the mysterious female;
This is the opening and closing
Mechanism of activity and passivity.
Coming and going over and over, never ceasing,
They alternate successively, without deviation.
A white-headed ancient
Rides off on a dragon,
A blue-eyed foreigner
Comes back on a tiger.
What is realized
As a result of the work?
Throughout sky and earth
The moonlight shines.

A Warning

Mere talk of Zen
Is vain boasting;
Extensive discourse and lofty talk
Take matters further afield.
It is like seeking reality
Through empty forms,
Like producing visual distortions

By rubbing the eyes.
Though you pursue things,
They're after all illusory;
Snap your head around,
And you arrive at home.
Don't blame me for talking so harshly—
Opening up the heart,
There should be no blockage.

Drawing Back from Error

Thirty-six hundred side-door methods—
Fixated people are befuddled by them;
Daily wasting attention
On reifying views,
When will they ever understand Life
And return to the root?
Why speak of exceptional attainment
Of intellectual brilliance?
Expertise in intellectual knowledge
Is not worth discussing.
All forms and names,
All external characterizations,
Ultimately amount to no more
Than so much mental gymnastics.

Countering Demons

How can torpor and drowsiness
Be prevented in meditation?
Do you see the ghost faces and spirit heads?
Torpor and distraction both
Stem from turbidity in energy;
Thoughts of objects continue
Because of such conditioning.
When the tide comes in,

The water comes up to the banks;
When the wind is still,
There are no waves on the river.
When essentially serene,
Feelings empty, mind unstirring,
There's no torpor or distraction
In meditation,
No demons in sleep.

Revealing the Correct

Active and passive practice are easy,
The medicine is not far away;
The arising of natural energy
Is like the ocean tide.
When you know how to gather
Both mercury and lead,
All material cravings
Then will pass away.
Overturn myriad existents
And the three bases join;
Refine away mundanities
And the five energies arrive.
Freeing the embryo in ten months,
The alchemy is complete;
The infant's form appears
And visits the spiritual firmament.

Harmonization

The three basic great medicines
Are will, mind, and body;
But if you fixate on will, mind, or body,
You are entangled in objects.
Tuning the breath requires tuning
The breath of the true breath;

Refining spirit calls for refining
The nonpsychological spirit.
On suddenly forgetting things and self,
The three flowers assemble;
On powerfully discarding impulses and objects,
The five energies arrive.
With thoroughly pervasive attainment,
There is no obstruction;
At all times, in all places,
One expresses Complete Reality.

Clarifying the Basis

Since the body is nonabsolute,
Labels are arbitrary;
Once there are labels,
The mind gets tangled up.
The waxing and waning of yin and yang
Polish present and past;
The rising and setting of sun and moon
Convey birth and death.
If you can maintain
Unified stability through time,
Then you'll know the stroke
Of midnight at noon.
Though dealing with the world
Is something that needs teaching,
The work of leaving the world
Must be clarified on your own.

Forging the Sword

An enlightened teacher taught me
To forge the blade of spirit;
What it all depends upon
Is the creative work of yin and yang.

Tempering the firmness of HEAVEN,
EARTH does the forging;
Fanning the fire of awareness
Is the wind of docility.
Having achieved unfailing concentration,
The mind-director is skilled;
Wiping out pernicious influences,
The will-general is valiant.
When eminent learners of Tao
Know the meaning of this,
It is easy for them
To shatter cosmic space.

The Moon Cave

The Moon Cave is clear and deep,
The environment most beautiful;
The one who dwells there
Makes a living upside down,
Refining the gold potion
In the jade furnace,
Cooking white snow sprouts
In the gold cauldron.
Operating the cosmic cycle,
Turning the handle of the Big Dipper,
Alternately passive and active,
Conveying the flow of energy,
Having passed through all the barriers
He freely sails the silver river in peace.

The Hut of Clarity

My hut is not an abode of idleness;
Ordinary people are not allowed
To see it on a whim.
A wife and husband make a living,

Three sons and three daughters
Form a group.
The world therein has always been vast;
The space outside is not really large.
If you ask the master what he does,
I reply that he faces south
To gaze at the north star.

POEMS EXTOLLING TRUE HAPPINESS

1.

Buddhas and immortals are all products
Of people of the world;
Nevertheless, those astray
Simply do not know.
Either they compete
Out of greed for fame,
Or else they rush around
In a struggle for profit.
Groaning and sweating
Under the burden of business,
Laboring busily
To support wives and children,
Even if you're prosperous
And have a beautiful wife,
None of it will accompany you
When you pass away.

2.

How can this compare
To Complete Reality, marvelous, unique?
Here is true happiness,
Known within one's heart.

The elixir comes from nonrefinement,
Refined in refinement;
The Tao goes to nondoing,
Done in doing.
Stopping thoughts, stopping entanglements,
Tune the generative energy;
Forget hearing, forget seeing,
Nurture the spiritual infant.
After the alchemical foundation
Is securely set up,
Five-colored light
Penetrates the curtains.

3.

Use EARTH for the furnace,
HEAVEN for the cauldron;
Penetrate the subtleties,
Comprehend inner design,
And you'll attain immortality.
It's all a matter of controlling sense
And returning it to essence—
This is cooking mercury
And mixing it with lead.
Stop compulsive involvements
And the pill of elixir glows;
Keep correct concentration complete,
And the jewel crystallizes.
This is the method
Of extraction and addition;
No need to worry anymore
Asking about the mystery.

4.

Active and passive practice are easy,
The medicines are not remote;

Creative evolution is just
Like the ocean tide.
The medicinal ingredients
Are just culled in nonbeing;
The fiery elixir is cooked
Wholly in concentration.
When the primordial and temporal conjoin,
All entanglements cease;
When the celestial and earthly commingle,
The five energies return to the source.
When obscurity is gone
And illumination is pure,
Then the work is done;
The true human emerges
And visits the spiritual sky.

5.

To refine the elixir,
First harmonize energy and spirit;
The water of reality
Is repeatedly poured on,
The fire of wisdom heats it.
Focus the spirit on energy,
Purify energy by stillness,
Preserve purity by attention;
Then sense, essence, and will
Join into one:
The primal celestial comes back,
Conditioned mundanity dissolves.
The golden furnace upright,
A thousand spirits meet;
The work in the cauldron complete,
Myriad forms pay court.
The medicine made, the elixir complete,
The spirit goes free;

The whole body emerges,
Now completely bared.

6.

The primordial ultimate spirit
Is subtle, hard to fathom;
Sense must be recovered,
Essence is always there.
Vitality and consciousness
Are divided into upper and lower;
The opening of the mysterious pass
Is right in the center.
When you know being is not being,
Then that is really being;
Understand voidness has no void,
And that is real voidness.
Nonbeing being, being nonbeing—
This is the very point;
The Great Sun glows scarlet
At the bottom of the billowing ocean.

7.

Serene, unstirring,
One merges with true eternity;
Dissolving all obscurities
Spontaneously restores light.
In stillness the will
Fosters the spiritual being;
In concentration consciousness
Weds unconditioned knowing.
Inwardly stable in the midst of peril, energy grows;
Action coming from calmness, vitality's ebullient.
In the silver river
There's not the slightest shadow;

The gold moon appears alone,
Shining with spiritual light.

8.

The marriage of the beautiful maid
To the metal man
Depends entirely on the work
Of the yellow woman to join them.
When husband and wife come together,
The clouds and rain of their feelings combine.
At leisure, they drink
In the mansion on the crimson hill;
Intoxicated, they sleep together
In the chamber of the purple climax.
Bliss in the evenings,
Happiness in the mornings,
Their sympathy is profound;
In a year they give birth to a baby.

9.

There are husband and wife
In everyone's body,
But the ignorant are too fixed on delusions—
Instead of seeking creative evolution within,
They set up alchemical foundations outside.
They mistakenly take arts of sexual intercourse
To be the "nine-cauldron" of the ancient sages.
It's hard for such animals to repent;
Before long death will come after them.

10.

I will tell you about
The husband and wife inside the body,
The blue-robed girl

137

And the white-haired old man:
When "metal" sense and "wood" essence combine,
Black mercury and red lead
Spontaneously commune sensitively.
Facing the moon and the breeze,
The spirit is free and blissful,
Producing endless clouds and rain.
If you can truly understand
This ultimate principle,
Crystallizing the embryo of reality
Is then a simple affair.

11.

The nine-restored, seven-reverted great elixir
Should be sought by learners in concentration.
When you truly understand the spiritual mechanism,
The two medicinal ingredients then combine:
Three years' development
Is completed in an instant,
The work of nine transformations
Is done in a trice.
Now you take the cauldron and furnace
And turn them over;
Then the light of the elixir
Shines through the spiritual isles.

12.

The unwritten transmission outside of doctrine
Is inherently complete in everyone.
The mystic breeze subtly clears the world,
The moon of wisdom beautifully stamps the hundred rivers.
Zen conundrums are all artificial metaphors;
Even direct pointing is still not the truth.

Conveying the experience which is before history
Is not in the Confucian circle of the absolute.

ALERTING THE WORLD ABOUT
THE FOUR CONDITIONS

Body, mind, society, events—
Four empty names:
How many confused people
Have been entangled by them!
Calamity and trouble come
From worldly power and materialism;
Vicious circles come
From obsession with objects.
In trackless serenity,
One may act at will;
Forgetting impulses when dealing with the world,
Let events change as they may.
When always letting go
In the midst of situations,
The foundation of life is secure,
Essence is complete and clear.

THE GOURD

The seed of spiritual illumination
Is produced primordially;
Stem firm, roots deep,
The principle is naturally so.
Daily add the soil
Of the state of EARTH;
Irrigate at proper times
With the spring in WATER.

139

When the flower opens, white jade,
It shines with light;
When the fruit forms, yellow gold,
It is round and firm.
On completion, the top of the head opens up;
Here there is another universe.

THE MIND MIRROR

Take the ore of HEAVEN
And put it in the furnace of EARTH;
The totality of space
Becomes a single pattern.
When the manifestation of reality is perfected,
It is round and radiant;
Where consciousness is polished,
It shines with being as is.
Emanating light, it pervades the universe;
Put into storage, it is a tiny pearl.
Raising it up clearly,
The Whole Body appears;
It's still necessary to break through
To merge with the essential axis.

THE MYSTERIOUS FEMALE

The door of the female of the mystic school
Is not hard to know;
Collect body and mind
And contemplate within.
When you understand the principle
Of alternation of the two modes,
Then you know the timing
Of coming and going of the one energy.

HEAVEN and EARTH, movement and stillness,
Open and close without cease;
FIRE and WATER, awareness and vitality,
Rise and descend, mixing and separating.
Set up the alchemical foundation
At the point where thought returns.

LEARNING

Chan Buddhism, Confucian Noumenalism,
The Taoism of Complete Reality—
Three schools of teaching were set up
To contact later people.
For Buddhists, elements are nonabsolute,
It's necessary to see the essence;
As Confucians investigate phenomena,
They must maintain sincerity.
On the Taoist's alchemical stand
Are kept points of fire;
All kinds of atoms are melted down
In the spiritual mansion.
When you understand all differences
Are resolved in one goal,
Then on the bright terrace
All is spring, inside and out.

VERSES ON FREEDOM

1.

On breaking through the opening of Chaos,
There are no Buddhas or Immortals.
This is no marvel outside mind,
And not mere verbal Zen.

I pass the days lightheartedly roaming,
And spend the nights freely sleeping.
Letting my body sink into the realm of the absolute,
I entrust all things to Heaven.

2.

All created phenomena
Are dust, without exception.
Comprehending the principles of things,
I let go of mind and body.
Wherever I am I rest in meditation,
At all times I delight in reality.
To waken the people of the world,
I always use the marrow of the *I Ching*.

3.

Reaching the subtlety of nondoing,
I don't go outside all day.
Impulsive involvements ended,
The celestial design remains.
In daily affairs,
The action of heaven is strong;
In everyday life,
The force of earth is calm.
I remind and suggest to my students—
Return to Life, go back to the root.

4.

Passing through all barriers,
One merges with the Great Sameness.
Tortoise hair is naturally always green,
The crane's crest is originally scarlet.
What can be verbalized is not the eternal Tao;

Work that is "done" is external work:
The true creative evolution
Is in profound abstraction.

5.

Having attained steadiness of body and mind,
I still the spirit and stabilize energy.
Body at ease, I transcend attachments;
Mind serene, I realize the uncreated.
Sun and moon come and go as they may,
HEAVEN and EARTH change freely.
Openness without obstruction
Reveals a unique great light.

6.

There is nothing special in my daily activities
But to maintain unified central truthfulness.
In stillness I tune my breathing;
In action I follow common sense.
Hiding my powers to assimilate to society,
I contain my light and do not show illumination.
In true freedom and bliss,
I'm ever calm and ever clear.

7.

As I serenely embrace nameless innocence,
Feelings about objects cannot invade.
As I fuse mercury and lead into powder,
Rubble turns to gold.
Seeing the ancient sages,
I reconcile Buddhism and Taoism.
Immediately opening, I transcend to reality,
Where there is no past and no present.

THE LAMP IN THE MIRROR

1.

The precious mirror is basically formless;
The lamp of communication emanates wisdom's light.
Being-as-such is fundamentally brilliantly clear;
The body of reality is originally radiant.
The gold cauldron burns with true fire,
The flower pond bathes the great light.
The true meaning herein
Is not apart from the center.

2.

In the quiet room I open the mirror of mind;
In the vacant hall I light the lamp of wisdom.
Outside is clear and bright,
Inside is effulgent light.
A tiny grain appears in the glow,
The silver moon is clear in the water.
In the gold crucible, suspended in space,
A grain of great elixir crystallizes.

EXTOLLING THE LOTUS

1.

One seed's spiritual sprout is different;
Others are not like it at all.
The spiritual body is fundamentally immaculate,
The true essence is basically pure.
The outward form is everywhere curved,
The holes within go all the way through.

144

Mud and mire cannot bog it down—
When it appears, the whole pond is red.

2.

Our original pure immaterial seed
Is crystal clear throughout all time.
Because it dislikes mental and material greed,
It bides for a time deep in the mud.
It always intends to help people out,
Ever determined to overcome selfishness.
Of the many who try to take it,
How many really know what it is?

BUILDING A HUT

1.

Choosing from the whole land of open nonreification,
I find suitable conditions in the jade capital.
In building the foundation,
It must be steady and stable;
In setting up the cauldron,
It must be thoroughly level.
Standing up the polar mountain as a pillar,
I set across it the absolute as the main beam.
The blue sky is the roof,
The occupant enjoys the uncreated.

2.

Leveling off the ground,
I finish the foundation the same day.
The mountains come in from the south,
The water flows out to the west.

145

The door is completely open,
The windows thoroughly clear.
Who are the companions in the hut?
The light of the moon,
The clarity of the breeze.

XX.

VEILED WORDS

Those who do not clearly understand are externally fixated on body, mind, society, and events; and they inwardly dwell on sensations, conceptions, actions, and consciousness. Therefore they change along with the world, are born and perish along with forms.

Buddhist literature says if people want to know all the Buddhas of past, present, and future, they should see that the natures of the world of phenomena are all created by mind. This means that when there is creation, then there is change; creation and change both derive from mind.

People all think that what creates and changes myriad beings is the fashioner of creation and change, but I do not agree. There is basically no fashioner of creation and change; beings create and change themselves. How is this so? All beings have mind, and it is because they have mind that there is creation and change. This is what I call self-creation and self-change.

The forms of all in the world that has form are originally nonexistent. Producing existence where there was none is called creation. When there is production, then there is destruction; when there is destruction, there is reversion to nonexistence. This is called change. Repeated creation and change is the norm for beings.

The essence of the unique reality is fundamentally existent; it exists but has no form, so it has no creation or change. This is the norm of the

Tao. People only know it has no creation or change, and think it does not create or change—they do not know there is great creation and change existing therein.

Who can know this without clear understanding? Those with clear understanding, those whose knowledge and wisdom are perfected, are able to see all phenomena as empty of absoluteness. Then the unified mind returns to tranquility, and lives independently in a transcendent state. Therefore there is no creation or change for them.

Those who do not clearly understand are externally fixated on body, mind, society, and events; and they inwardly dwell on sensations, conceptions, actions, and consciousness. Therefore they change along with the world, are born and perish along with forms.

What the eye sees is called form; received in the mind, it is called sensation. Once taken into the mind in the form of a mental picture, it is called conception. When conception continues, it leads to doing; this is called action. The result of action, conforming to the good or bad nature of the action, is called conditioned consciousness. The flurry of conditioned consciousness is the root of routine existence. Thus it is impossible to get out of creation and change.

Anyone who is not bound by illusory objects, not defiled by the impact of phenomena, not obstructed by wandering feelings, and not afflicted by craving, will then be able to see forms, sensations, conceptions, actions, and conditioned consciousness as empty of ultimate reality. Since these are empty, how can there be creation and change? This is what the Buddhists call the ineffable mind of nirvana.

Taoist literature says being and nonbeing produce one another. That is, nonbeing produces being—this is creation; being produces nonbeing—this is change.

Taoist literature also says, "Effecting ultimate openness, keeping utterly quiet, as myriad things act in concert, I thereby watch the return." That is, watching return is knowing change; if you know change, you do not change, and if you do not change, how can there be creation?

Who can reach this but those who see clearly, without obstruction?

Those of clear perception, pure and illumined, can see that body, mind, society, and events exist in insubstantial illusion. Existence makes things and beings, which revert to insubstantial illusions once they have reached their culmination.

Those who see in this way know the formless form is the true form. Because they nurture the formless form, they always preserve the body-less body, and so they keep reality complete. When one is unadulterated, pure, completely whole, there is a merging with the infinite; in undiffer-entiated vastness, there is a merging with the unparalleled. Transcending even beyond open nothingness, this is called freedom from creation and change.

People with fixations are physically and mentally unsettled; assailed by thoughts and worries, they therefore lose the formless and the body-less, and so they flow in the waves of birth and death, always sunk in the sea of suffering.

If you can collect body and mind, set aside thoughts and worries, not let inner states out, not let external objects in, and be inwardly and out-wardly clear and serene, this is called clarification. When you get to the point where you inwardly forget the mind and outwardly forget the body, so that the unique reality is clear and you are like cosmic space, open and unobstructed, how can there be any creation or change therein?

Confucian literature says, "Not envying, not seeking, no blame, no complicity." Not envying and not seeking means not being subject to creation; no blame and no complicity means not being subject to change.

The Connected Sayings commentary in the *I Ching* says, "At a dis-tance, find it in things; nearby, find it in yourself." I say that "at a distance, find it in things" means you know all objects are insubstantial and tem-porary; "nearby, find it in yourself" means you know the physical and mental elements are all empty of ultimate reality.

By outwardly being aloof of all objects and inwardly detached from the physical and mental elements, you can accord with the celestial workings, be pleased with heaven, know the beginning and end of things, know the reason of the hidden and the obvious, know the explanation of life and death, find out truth, fulfill human nature, and arrive at the purpose of life. Because of being pleased with heaven, you do not worry; because of fulfilling nature, you do not doubt.

Who can reach this but those who achieve knowledge? Those who accomplish knowledge are sincere, lucid, calm, and stable; so they know that illusory forms continually arise and pass away, that the deluded mind is discriminatory and partial, that society and the times shift and change uncertainly, and that works perish and do not last.

When the refinement brought about through observation is thoroughly mature, this is called the accomplishment of sages. Because it is permeated by unity, there is no creation or change.

If you do not accomplish knowledge, you cannot determine the character of things; if you cannot determine things, you change and shift along with things—then where are essence and life?

If there is fluid movement, not fixated, circulating throughout space, heaven and earth then meet in oneself, myriad things are complete in oneself. When you return to vision of the heart of heaven, myriad existents return to open nonreification; then creation and change cease.

Metaphorically speaking, if HEAVEN and EARTH do not move fluidly, sun and moon do not travel—then where are the combinations of yin and yang? If yin and yang do not interact, they do not ascend and descend—then how can myriad beings exist? The bodies of HEAVEN and EARTH are pure and unified; because they do not mix the aberrant with the true, and do not change, therefore there is no creation and no change.

The creation of creationless creation is great creation, the change of changeless change is great change. Those who see this thereby know that all things and beings in the world are temporary compounds, and that the operations of yin and yang are all illusions. Who but the most fluid in the world can keep up with this?

Viewing the matter in this way, we can see that the three teachings— Buddhism, Taoism, and Confucianism—are just a matter of mind: creation and change depend on mind, and transcendence of creation and change also depends on mind.

In learning Buddhism, it is essential to see essence. To see essence, it is first necessary to remove habit-conditioned energy by means of certainly stabilized will, and to preserve clear lucidity by the power of strict observation. After that, see through all kinds of vain illusory mental states, and do not fixate on things, so that thoughts do not follow feelings.

Thoughts are the root of affliction, mental states are the seeds of reification. When thoughts arise, all afflictions arise; when thoughts cease, all afflictions cease. When mental states are produced, all sorts of reifications are produced; when mental states pass away, all sorts of reifications pass away. When thoughts arise, stop them—all come from mind. When you reach the point where "arising and passing away itself passes away, and quiescence is bliss," this is seeing essence.

Students today who cannot see essence are hindered by two obstructions, abstract and concrete. Abstract obstructions cannot be dissolved but by great perception; concrete obstructions cannot be dissolved but by great cessation. Great perception means cutting through by knowledge; great cessation means controlling by power.

When cutting through by knowledge is perfected, all abstractions are empty of absoluteness; when controlling by power is perfected, all concretizations are empty of absoluteness. When you realize the great emptiness of emptiness and the ultimate reality of reality, this is the consummation of great perception. Then thoughts and emotional consciousness of body, mind, society, and events all stop at once; this is the consummation of great cessation.

Learning Taoism is a matter of preserving essence. To preserve essence, it is first necessary to cut through delusions with the sword of wisdom, dissolve attachment to sense experience by maximizing the transcendent primordial consciousness and minimizing the temporally conditioned consciousness, and to use the power of concentration to forget feelings, cut off rumination, remove psychological burdens, and clarify the mind.

When the mind is clear, burdens removed, rumination ended, and feelings forgotten, this is called preserving essence. When the true essence is present, there is no creation or change.

Students today get carried away by emotional consciousness. If you want to get rid of emotional consciousness, first get rid of the fluctuating mind. When the mind does not fluctuate, then the body does not fluctuate.

Getting rid of the fluctuating mind begins with having no thoughts. When you have fully developed the habit of freedom from thought, you can reach a state of serene concentration free from dreams and thoughts. When this is fully developed, you can reach a state free from conception.

Freedom from dreams is important for the present; freedom from conception is important at the end of life. Free from conception, you do not create; free from dreams, you do not change. Not creating, not changing, you are not born and do not die.

The essence of the study of Confucianism lies in fulfilling human nature. Fulfilling human nature is a matter of clarifying enlightened qualities and resting in ultimate good. After you know where to rest, then you have stability; when you have stability, you can forget things and self.

The statement on the hexagram MOUNTAIN in the *I Ching* says, "Stopping at the back, you don't find the body; walking in the garden, you don't see the person. No blame." Stopping at the back means forgetting oneself; walking in the garden not seeing the person means forgetting things. Knowing how and where to stop—therefore being able to forget things and self and so to keep the celestial design intact—is called fulfilling human nature.

When people today cannot fulfill human nature, it is because of burdens of body and mind. Once there are burdens, there is blockage. It is necessary to apply firm decisiveness and effective resolution. By being firm and decisive you can forget things; by being effectively resolute you can forget self. When things and self are forgotten, you will surely fulfill human nature and arrive at the meaning of life.

I observe that most people in the world think this body has a self in it. This reveals a serious lack of reflection. As this body exists due to creation, did it have a form before it was created, did it have a name, did it have a self? After it has changed, does it have a form, does it have a name, does it have a self? Since none of these exist either before or after, how can we cling to reification of self only in the interval between?

People do not realize that body, mind, the world, and events are fundamentally unreal in an ultimate sense; when we try to find past, present, and future, ultimately we cannot grasp them. The past has disappeared, the present changes from moment to moment, the future is uncertain.

Throughout the ages people have fixated on unreal objects in the midst of dreamlike illusion, forming the seeds of repetitious life cycles. Therefore they are born and die without hope of release.

If, on the other hand, people in the midst of these dreamlike illusory objects can experientially know them for what they are, and thus can dissolve fixations, they can reach enlightenment.

One day I brought up this issue for my students to look into. Two or three of them understood to some extent, so I composed this essay for them, to convey mind by mind.

If you can realize directly, inwardly understand and tacitly comprehend, then you know how and where to stop, not recounting the past, not worrying about the future, not being attached to the present. When these three are combined, you attain great independence, you roam freely in the ocean of tranquility, wander in the homeland of nothing-whatsoever, float in the realm of contentment.

When you get to this point, you will know that creation and change have no power over you. But there is still something yet higher. Tell me, what do you call that which is higher? Turn over the legs of nothingness, smash cosmic space to smithereens, and only then will you be done.

Design by David Bullen
Typeset in Mergenthaler Bembo
by Wilsted & Taylor
Printed by Maple-Vail
on acid-free paper